The Inclusive Early Childhood Educator

The Inclusive Early Childhood Educator

A Hands-On Approach

**DR JANE WARREN
& BLAKE STEWART**

Published in 2025 by Amba Press, Melbourne, Australia
www.ambapress.com.au

© Jane Warren and Blake Stewart 2025

All rights reserved. No part of this book may be reproduced or transmitted in any form or by any means, electronic or mechanical, including photocopying, recording or by any information storage and retrieval system, without prior permission in writing from the publisher.

Cover design: Tess McCabe
Editor: Rica Dearman

ISBN: 9781923215726 (pbk)
ISBN: 9781923215733 (ebk)

A catalogue record for this book is available from the National Library of Australia.

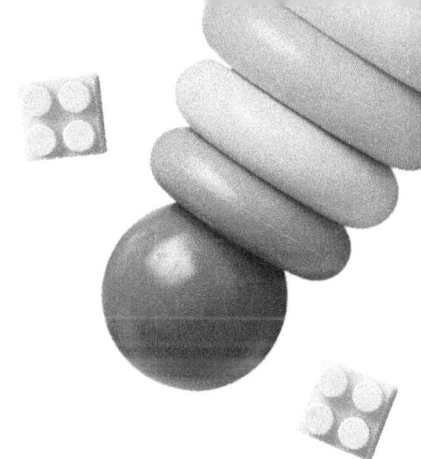

Acknowledgement

We would like to acknowledge the children with disabilities, developmental delays or neurodivergence and their families that we have had, and continue to have, the privilege of working with. Being able to share your lived experience and unique perspectives has shaped our understanding and enriched our practice. Not only has it made us better educators, but the knowledge we have gained through learning alongside you has created a ripple effect – spreading beyond our own work to influence others in the sector, fostering more inclusive and responsive approaches.

This book would not have been possible without the opportunities we have gained from learning from you all, and we are deeply grateful.

Preface

Our goal is to give you practical ideas, supported by best practice research. It would be great to be able to say that this book will give you all the answers about becoming an inclusive early childhood educator, but unfortunately, that isn't the case! Instead, we are hoping to share our collective years of experience and knowledge to empower you to take your practice to the next level.

We have been teachers in early childhood education and care (ECEC) services and have each had our fair share of successes and challenges. Working in an early childhood service is an exceptionally rewarding and privileged career. The opportunity to engage with children and families and contribute to positive outcomes is a gift. However, when we are faced with children whose abilities and diversity may not follow our current knowledge and expectations, we can feel overwhelmed, or unsure how to support the child appropriately. Both of us have pursued postgraduate studies in supporting children with disabilities, developmental delays and neurodivergence because we wanted to be better positioned to meet these challenges and support all children during their important early childhood years.

Being an inclusive educator needs to come from within. Children with disabilities, developmental delays or neurodivergence are children first. All children deserve and need opportunities to have fun. They deserve to be engaged. They have the right to be active participants in their own lives. If you are not grounded in the belief that everyone should have opportunities, and everyone needs to feel valued, it doesn't matter how much you learn, or how much you know.

Sometimes we can have the best intentions and really want to make a difference but are struggling to know how to do that. This book is designed to provide a whole range of information and strategies to help you take small steps to becoming an inclusive educator. We hope you will share this with your colleagues and contribute to building communities where difference is celebrated, and every child is truly valued for their uniqueness.

Table of contents

Introduction — 1

Chapter 1: Inclusion and why we do it — 7
Chapter 2: Getting to know each child — 17
Chapter 3: Having targeted conversations with families — 35
Chapter 4: A collaborative, integrated approach — 49
Chapter 5: Stocking your toolbox — 69
Chapter 6: Building confidence and capacity in your team — 93
Chapter 7: Supporting transitions — 105

Conclusion — 119
Useful resources — 121
References — 123
About the authors — 127

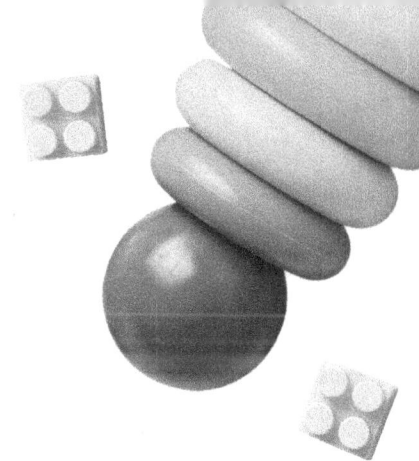

Introduction

Early childhood is a critical period in children's lives. There is a significant amount of research that supports the importance of the first five years and the impact the first 2,000 days have on the trajectory of learning, development and wellbeing (Doyle, 2020; National Scientific Council on the Developing Child, 2007). Early childhood educators have an important role in the lives of young children, and early childhood service settings are critical environments in which all children can be supported to thrive. Early childhood services are diverse, and all children should feel a sense of belonging within their service. The Early Years Learning Framework (EYLF) is part of the National Quality Framework within Australia and provides principles, practices and outcomes which guide consistent quality practice across all early childhood services. The EYLF states, "In early childhood, and throughout life, trusting relationships and affirming experiences are crucial to a sense of belonging. Belonging is central to being and becoming in that it shapes who children are and who they can become" (AGDE, 2022, p.6).

While early childhood services may provide quality practice, it is important to ensure that *all* children have equitable opportunities to participate and be engaged. This text has been developed to support educators to be inclusive, with a particular focus on children with disabilities, developmental delays or neurodivergence. Remember that the principles of inclusion need to underpin our approach to all children and families. There is, however, something important we need to think about before we get started – change.

Language

Please keep in mind that terminology, language and practice can and will change. This text is written using current terminology that exists at the time of publication. If this text was written five, 10 or 20 years ago, different terminology would have been used that was reflective of current expectations and knowledge. But not all terminology that was acceptable in 2004 is still applicable today. For example, in the early 2000s, the term 'additional needs' was most widely accepted as the terminology used for disabilities, developmental delays and neurodivergence. However, since then, it has been acknowledged that this is more of an umbrella term which encompasses a wide range of diversity, including but not limited to, cultural and linguistic diversity, Aboriginal and Torres Strait Islanders, children experiencing trauma and individuals with complex health needs. The term 'additional needs' also implied that people with disabilities, developmental delays or neurodivergence had 'extra' needs. What is more correct is that they may require additional support to have their rightful needs met.

In Australia, both person-first and identity-first language are used to refer to people with a disability, or disabled people. Everyone should be respectful and affirm the preferences of each individual. Person-first language refers to language where a person is put before the disability and recognises disabilities as just one part of a person, such as a person with cerebral palsy, for example. Identity-first language, such as an autistic person or deaf person, is used by many as a recognition of their disability as them, without being able to, or wanting to, separate that as just one part of them. Most people with a disability have very strong preferences regarding the use of either identity-first or person-first language, and non-disabled people need to be led by, respect and affirm the preferences of each individual person with a disability.

People with Disability Australia (PWDA) does not support the use of euphemisms, such as 'handicapable', 'differently abled', 'special needs' or 'living with disability', to refer to people with disabilities (PWDA, 2019, p.9). One thing that is crucial is that we avoid negative terminology, such as 'victim' or 'sufferer', as these reinforce stereotypes that people with disabilities are unhappy and should be recipients of pity. While some people may argue that they are just words, negative terminology is disempowering, discriminatory, degrading and offensive. We have chosen to use person-first language within this text as our experience with many families of young children with disabilities, developmental delays or neurodivergence have indicated this as their preference.

Early intervention

Let's start by thinking about what early intervention actually is. Traditionally, the term 'early intervention' was seen as something that was done 'to' people and can be a term that can trigger a negative emotional response. Consider the Stolen Generation. People outside families intervened to make decisions they felt would be best for families. We know how detrimental this was – not just to individuals involved at the time, but it led to generational trauma for so many people. However, when we refer to early intervention in this chapter, we are referring to collaborating with people as early as possible to provide the best opportunities for maximum outcomes. As stated by Reimagine, "Early childhood intervention is the term used to describe the service and supports that children and their families receive during the early years, when the child is developing most rapidly" (Reimagine Australia, 2024).

Early intervention works most effectively in natural environments for children, and it is important to remember that early childhood education (ECE) is, in itself, early intervention. It is not separate – but rather the ideal, naturalistic setting to provide those opportunities for children to work towards maximum outcomes.

Overview of text

No text is going to provide you with all the answers. But we believe that sharing experiences, research and knowledge will provide some foundational information, points to ponder and support you to reflect on your own practice. We will explore several topics that continue to challenge educators working in early childhood services.

Each chapter unpacks different areas that will support quality inclusive practice. We begin looking at the bigger picture of what inclusion really is and why it is essential and should never be seen as optional. Subsequent chapters address specific practices of how to really get to know each child, and how to have targeted conversations with families when there are concerns regarding a child's development. We then unpack what an integrated approach to early intervention looks like, specific strategies that become part of your 'toolbox' to draw upon and how to build confidence and capacity in your team. The final chapter addresses important transitions and how to support children transitioning into your service, daily transitions and transition out of your service. Each chapter has key takeaway points, reflective questions you can use for professional learning in your team and some useful resources you may want to use.

If you are new to the sector, or feel unprepared to really be inclusive, we hope this gives you a strong starting point. If you are already an inclusive educator, we hope this affirms your practice. One step in the right direction is one step you can take to make a difference – not just for a child with disabilities, developmental delays or neurodivergence and their family, but ultimately, a difference to everyone as you work together across your service to value and respect every individual and become more inclusive community members.

Key terms

Here are some key terms, along with their meanings, that are used throughout this book and within ECE:

Developmental assessment	This is used to assess children's development across several areas, such as communication, social skills, cognition, motor skills, behaviour and functional self-help skills.
Developmental delay	Developmental delay is literally a delay in a child's development. This can be short term or a sign of a long-term concern.
Developmental screening	"Developmental screening is the practice of systematically looking for and monitoring signs that a young child may be delayed in one or more areas of development. Screening is not meant to establish a diagnosis for the child, but rather to help professionals determine whether more in-depth assessment is the next step. In most cases, screening rules out the likelihood that further assessment is needed" (Squires & Bricker, 2009).
Disability	In Australia, disability is defined as "long-term physical, mental health, intellectual, neurological or sensory differences which, in interaction with various attitudinal and environmental barriers, may hinder full and effective participation in society on an equal basis with others" (Australian Disability Network, 2024).
Early childhood supports (intervention)	Early childhood supports (intervention) refers to a range of services and supports for children with disabilities, developmental delays or neurodivergence, including supports to optimise children's development, strengthen capacity of families in supporting their child, and promote inclusion and participation of children and their families in community.

Early identification	Early identification is not about diagnosis, but instead an evaluation of a young child who is at risk or suspected of having disabilities, developmental delays or neurodivergence.
Individualised Education Plans (IEP)	Individualised Education Plans (IEPs), otherwise known as Inclusion Support Plans, are tailored documents that outline specific strategies and goals for children with disabilities, developmental delays or neurodivergence.
Neuro-affirming	Neuro-affirming means supporting and accepting people's unique neurological differences. It involves creating positive and inclusive environments that recognise and value different ways of thinking and behaving.
Neurodivergence	Neurodivergence is a non-medical term that is used to describe anyone whose brain is formed or works differently to the typical brain, and those who experience the world differently to others.
Neurodiversity	Neurodiversity refers to the variety of ways that people's brains can work. It recognises that brain differences, like those seen in autism, attention deficit hyperactivity disorder and other differences, exist and should be respected.

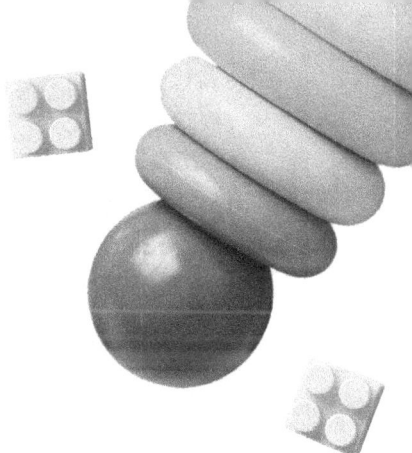

Chapter 1

Inclusion and why we do it

What is inclusion?

When we think of inclusion in relation to education, and specifically ECE, the focus is on ensuring that all children are welcomed and valued, have equitable opportunities to participate, and be engaged. This reference is usually to those seen as being from diverse populations, such as those with cultural diversity, Aboriginal and Torres Strait Islander children, and those with disabilities, developmental delays or neurodivergence.

You will notice that we use the term 'diverse populations' rather than 'disadvantaged groups'. This is intentional, as we believe that the term 'disadvantaged' goes against what we see as inclusion. The focus of this text is inclusion of children with disabilities, developmental delays and neurodivergence.

Let's first consider some ideas around inclusion. Sometimes the term inclusion is used synonymously with integration or assimilation, but these have very different meanings.

Integration – where children with disabilities, developmental delays or neurodivergence are enrolled into an early childhood service alongside their typically developing peers. However, the expectation is really for the child with disabilities, developmental delays or neurodivergence to adapt to the environment and expectation.

Assimilation – where children with disabilities, developmental delays or neurodivergence are in the service alongside their typically developing peers but they are expected to become 'like the others' – losing their own identity and individuality.

Inclusion – traditionally, when this term was first used, it was more focused on 'including' a child with disabilities, developmental delays or neurodivergence – seemingly placing some of this responsibility on the child. But since then, we have realised that inclusion is not about one child, but rather, focuses on the whole environment. "Inclusion focuses on the whole environment and making changes to it so that all children can participate. In an inclusive environment diversity is acknowledged, respected and viewed as a resource for learning, growth and change" (Reimagine Australia, 2024). Inclusion is fundamentally a human right, where each person is valued for their own individuality. According to Reimagine Australia, "Inclusion is a right – and every child has a right to be included and to participate in their community. Inclusion happens when children are viewed as capable and valued contributors as opposed to having deficits that need to be fixed" (2024).

Early Childhood Australia has also developed a position statement on inclusion; it states: "Inclusion ensures that all children participate meaningfully while learning and interacting in programs that acknowledge each child's strengths and interests, so that they are supported to be active members of their community" (2016, p.2). It focuses on three dimensions: access, participation and outcomes.

Inclusion is not just about the child with disabilities, developmental delays or neurodivergence, but for everyone to embrace diversity and value everyone as unique individuals. It is about making a difference to a child with disabilities, developmental delays or neurodivergence, and everyone within the whole service becoming more inclusive individuals, learning and growing alongside each other. "Inclusion benefits everybody and makes a difference not just for now, but for the future" (Reimagine Australia, 2024).

Figure 1: Inclusion in early childhood

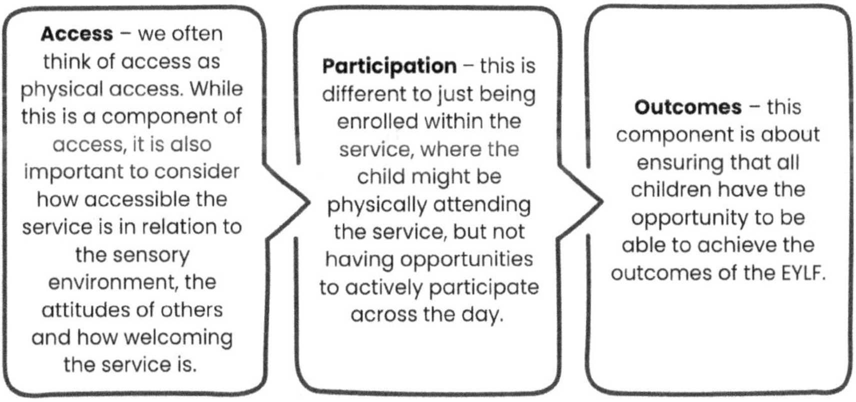

Access – we often think of access as physical access. While this is a component of access, it is also important to consider how accessible the service is in relation to the sensory environment, the attitudes of others and how welcoming the service is.

Participation – this is different to just being enrolled within the service, where the child might be physically attending the service, but not having opportunities to actively participate across the day.

Outcomes – this component is about ensuring that all children have the opportunity to be able to achieve the outcomes of the EYLF.

Legislation and conventions underpinning inclusion

Across the world there are laws and conventions which support inclusion, such as the United Nations Convention on the Rights of the Child and United Nations Convention on the Rights of Persons with Disabilities.

United Nations Convention on the Rights of the Child (UNCRC)

The UNCRC (United Nations, 1989) is the most ratified international treaty, with the United States being the only country in the United Nations not to have signed. As a signatory, Australia has committed its responsibility to uphold the rights of all children. While all the rights are applicable to *all* children, Article 2 focuses specifically on rights and respect, without discrimination. "Article 2 (Non-discrimination): The Convention applies to *all children*, whatever their race, religion or abilities; whatever they think or say, whatever type of family they come from. It doesn't matter where children live, what language they speak, what their parents do, whether they are boys or girls, what their culture is, whether they have a disability or whether they are rich or poor. No child should be treated unfairly on any basis" (United Nations, 1989).

United Nations Convention on the Rights of Persons with Disabilities (UNCRPD)

The purpose of the UNCRPD is to "promote, protect and ensure the full and equal enjoyment of all human rights and fundamental freedoms by all persons with disabilities, and to promote respect for their inherent dignity" (Australian Human Rights Commission, n.d.). Again, as a signatory, Australia has committed to ensuring that all children with disabilities have the same rights and freedoms that every other child does. This is not about additional rights for children with disabilities – but about ensuring that all rights of the child are afforded to children who have disabilities as well as those who do not.

Disability Discrimination Act

Within Australia, the Disability Discrimination Act (DDA) was developed in 1992 as a significant piece of legislation that makes it unlawful to discriminate against anyone because of a disability. While the DDA applies to people of all ages with disabilities, it supports the information addressed within the UNCRC and UNCRPD, to ensure that no child is discriminated against.

How inclusion links to the National Quality Framework

Inclusion and the National Quality Framework

In 2012, Australia released its first National Quality Framework for early childhood services, to ensure consistent quality across all early childhood services within Australia. It contains laws, regulations, standards and learning frameworks. But how does this important framework relate to inclusion?

The National Quality Framework was designed to improve education and care services across Australia, with a particular focus on lifting the baseline of what is seen as acceptable. The laws and regulations outline what legal obligations apply to approved providers, nominated supervisors and educators. The law sets the national standard, and the regulations support the law across a range of operational areas.

The National Quality Standard (NQS) sets a high national benchmark for quality. There are seven different quality areas, and while these do not all specifically apply to inclusion, they all relate. The seven areas are:

1. Educational program and practice
2. Children's health and safety
3. Physical environment
4. Staffing arrangements
5. Relationships with children
6. Collaborative partnerships with families and communities
7. Governance and leadership.

For assessment and rating, services are assessed against these seven quality areas. Within the quality areas, there is still flexibility to reflect on what you see as quality practice. The examples below relate to inclusion and respect for diversity:

> *QA1 – 1.1.2 – Child-centred: "Each child's current knowledge, strengths, ideas, culture, abilities and interests are the foundation of the program"*
>
> *QA3 – 2.3.1 – Inclusive environment: "Outdoor and indoor spaces are organised and adapted to support every child's participation and to engage every child in quality experiences in both built and natural environments"*
>
> *QA5 – 5.2.2 – Self-regulation: "Each child is supported to regulate their own behaviour, respond appropriately to the behaviour of others and communicate effectively to resolve conflicts"*

(ACECQA, 2018b)

Early Years Learning Framework (EYLF)

The EYLF was developed in 2009 (DEEWR, 2009) and updated in 2022 (AGDE, 2022). This framework is designed to support educators, teachers and early childhood providers to enrich children's learning through collaborating with children, families, other professionals, schools and community members to inform the educational programs and practices of the service. The EYLF sees children as capable, competent, confident and active members of their communities and lifelong learners. The three key pillars of the EYLF are Belonging, Being and Becoming, and guide connections across the framework between principles, practices and learning outcomes.

Figure 2: The three key pillars of the EYLF

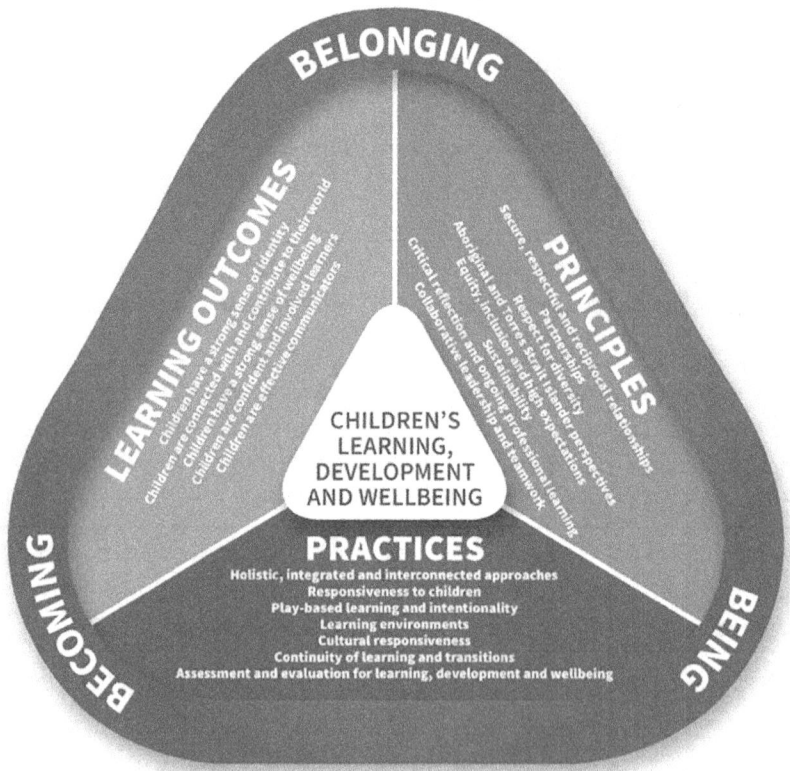

(ADGE, 2022)

Again, this framework is not specifically tailored to children with disabilities, developmental delays or neurodivergence. However, it *is* tailored to *all* children, so clearly applies to children with disabilities, developmental delays or neurodivergence. If you unpack each of the principles, practices or learning outcomes, you can see some relate very specifically to inclusion, such as:

Principles	• Respect for diversity
	• Equity, inclusion and high expectations
Practices	• Responsiveness to children
	• Play-based learning and intentionality
Learning outcomes	• Outcome 1: Children have a strong sense of identity
	• Outcome 4: Children are confident and involved learners

(ADGE, 2022)

These are just examples of those more explicitly related, but educators must remember that every principle, practice and learning outcome is relevant to children with disabilities, developmental delays and neurodivergence, and to those without.

Enrolment vs inclusion

Enrolment in an early childhood service is a great starting point, but in itself is not inclusive. Of course, being accepted into a service is important, but if there are no inclusive practices, this can be more exclusionary for a child than not being in the service at all. Inclusion is about making changes to the service to ensure a child is included – for example, if a child finds bright lights overwhelming, you can minimise this sensory input to make it easier for the child and allow them to be more fully included. As stated earlier, inclusion focuses on making changes to the whole environment so that all children can participate.

Philosophy > policy > practice

Your service philosophy should reflect the collective beliefs, vision and values that guide your program and practice, and inclusion should be a key component. A shared philosophy is important, so everyone is on 'the same page'. When everyone agrees on the philosophy, you have a much better chance to work in a positive direction. This should not be limited to educators, but also management and families. It is important to consider:

- What you want to achieve in relation to inclusion
- Why you all believe this is important
- How you can make small steps to working toward your overall goals.

Once you are all happy with the philosophy, you can start translating this into policies which will inform your practice. Policies give you a framework for decision-making, and guide consistent, quality practice. These are also important so that families understand what happens in the service, and the reasons (philosophy) that underpin the policies.

Let's consider your inclusion policy. It will be informed by what you believe about inclusion, but will then outline information that gives you specific guidance as to how you can support your philosophy. Your practices then need to align to the policies of the service. Let's look at this with an example.

Figure 3: Philosophy, policies and practices

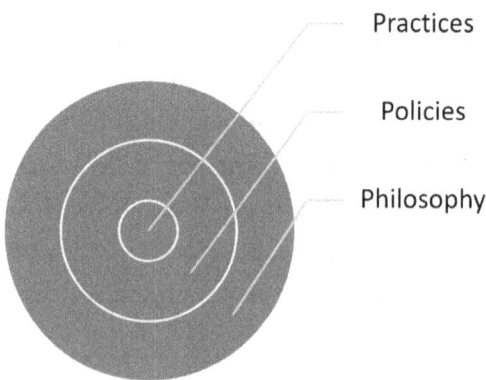

Your philosophy might state:	*Your policy might state:*	*Your practices should include:*
All children are respected as unique individuals, and diversity is celebrated.	We will ensure that all children have the opportunity to access all learning experiences and equitably participate in the program.	• Considering how to modify equipment and resources to make them accessible to all children • Reflecting on the sensory environment and reducing overstimulating light and sound to assist children who are overwhelmed by the current environment • Looking at aspects of the routine to consider what realistic but high expectations are currently appropriate for each child • Making modifications to enable all children to have the opportunity to participate • Celebrating difference within all aspects of your service to set up a culture of inclusion • Continually seeking to understand and honour each child's felt sense of safety and belonging.

Key takeaways

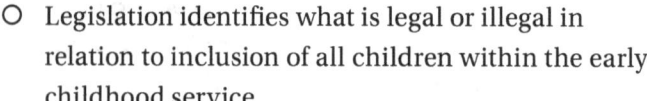

- Legislation identifies what is legal or illegal in relation to inclusion of all children within the early childhood service.
- There are guiding conventions and documents that support ethical decision-making around children who are diverse learners.
- Remember that the NQS and EYLF must guide your practice with *all* children, irrespective of disabilities, developmental delays or neurodivergence.
- Celebrating all children as unique individuals must be part of your philosophy, policies and ultimately your daily practice within the service.

Reflective questions for professional learning

- Consider how inclusive your service is. What strategies do you use in your service to demonstrate inclusion?
- Why is it important to consider the UNCRC and UNCRPD in your service?
- Think about the NQS. For each of the standards, select one of the criteria under each area and discuss how it relates to inclusion.

Chapter 2

Getting to know each child

Building relationships

Relationships are the foundation for quality ECEC services and are explicitly stated as one of the core principles underpinning the EYLF. These principles "reflect contemporary theories, perspectives and research evidence concerning children's learning and early childhood pedagogy" (AGDE, 2022, p.14). While this principle of "Secure, respectful and reciprocal relationships" (AGDE, 2022, p.14) focuses primarily on relationships between educators and children, relationships within early childhood education and care (ECEC) services extend far beyond this – and include relationships with families, colleagues and wider community. To really get to know a child, we need to build a secure relationship with them but also have discussions with children's families and other educators working alongside the children.

This chapter explores how we can reach a genuine understanding of individual children. This is not just part of our responsibility as educators but also plays an important role when we feel a child may require additional support within and outside the service. (This will be explored further in Chapter 3.)

Understanding child development

A deep understanding of child development is a crucial foundation for early childhood educators. This knowledge enables educators to effectively support and guide each child's unique learning journey, ensuring that children are met where they are developmentally, and encouraged to grow at their own pace. Early childhood is a period of rapid and varied growth, and a strong grasp of developmental theories and milestones is essential for recognising when children are progressing typically and when they may need additional support. There are a number of developmental milestone documents, with many educators being most familiar with the EYLF Developmental Milestones (2018a). This foundation allows educators to make informed decisions about how best to adapt teaching strategies and learning environments to provide both appropriate challenges and necessary scaffolding for each child's development.

The importance of child development knowledge becomes particularly evident when educators encounter children at different stages of development. For instance, take Sam, a one-year-old who has not yet begun to walk. While walking typically begins between nine and 18 months, Sam's current developmental stage is not unusual. Knowing this, an educator can confidently support Sam's motor development by offering activities that encourage strength and balance, such as playing with push toys or engaging in safe climbing exercises. With an understanding of child development, educators can offer experiences that meet Sam where he is, fostering his gross motor skills in a developmentally appropriate way.

Now consider Sarah, a four-year-old who is also not walking. It is unusual for a child of this age not to be walking and this may signal health or developmental concern. At this age, most children have developed strong gross motor skills, including walking, running and climbing. The fact that Sarah is not walking at the age of four requires more in-depth attention and intervention. For educators, understanding the developmental expectations for Sarah's age group is critical. This knowledge enables them to identify that her needs may go beyond the early childhood centre's support and require collaboration with doctors who have child development expertise (for example, paediatricians) and allied health professionals (like physiotherapists or occupational therapists). By working closely with Sarah's family and health professionals, educators can collaboratively develop and implement a tailored plan that addresses her specific needs, ensuring she receives the right support for her physical development.

These examples highlight the critical role a solid foundation in understanding child development plays in the work of early childhood educators. Without this understanding, it would be difficult to discern when a child is progressing at their own pace versus when further support is needed. Child development knowledge empowers educators to provide the right support at the right time, ensuring that children like Sam, who is still on track, and Sarah, who may need more support, receive the guidance and resources they need to thrive. This foundation is not just about tracking milestones – it's about responding to each child's unique developmental trajectory with informed, compassionate and proactive care.

Observe – using a wide range of styles

Observation is one of the most powerful tools in ECE, offering educators valuable insights into each child's development, learning style and needs. However, the key to effective observation lies in choosing the right method for each child and situation. Every child is unique, with their own abilities, strengths and challenges, so it's important to adapt observation styles accordingly. Traditional methods can be useful, but a flexible approach is essential, particularly when working with children with disabilities, developmental delays or neurodivergence.

Take Sarah, the four-year-old from our last example, who is not yet walking. Using a standard four-year-old physical development checklist is not the best approach, since it focuses on milestones like running and jumping – skills that Sarah has not yet have developed. Instead, a more personalised method, such as anecdotal records, could be used to document her social interactions or problem-solving abilities during play. By focusing on her strengths, educators can gain a clearer picture of Sarah's development without relying solely on physical milestones.

Now consider Sam, the one-year-old who has not yet started walking. Using time sampling during playtime might be more appropriate in his case, as it allows educators to observe his motor skills at different points throughout the day. In a time sample observation, an educator makes a brief jotting observation of a child at regular scheduled intervals (maybe every 10 minutes) over a set period of time – maybe an hour or two of free play. It is an observation method that allows the educator to see the activity the child is engaged in, as well as ways a child is involved at a particular time. This approach can help educators and his family understand Sam's current developmental stage and decide if additional support is needed.

These examples show how different observation styles can be tailored to each child's specific situation, ensuring that assessments are meaningful and relevant.

When observing children with disabilities, developmental delays or neurodivergence, selecting observation methods that align with their abilities is critical. For instance, a physical development checklist might be less relevant for a child with physical disabilities. Instead, using photographic or video observations could provide a better understanding of how the child engages in communication or social activities. These visual tools allow educators to track progress over time and focus on the child's strengths, highlighting what they can do rather than dwelling on limitations.

It is also important to note that observations without analysis and interpretation are not very useful. Simply recording what children do, without reflecting on the significance of their behaviours or actions, limits the value of the observation. Educators must take the time to interpret what they see – what might the child's behaviour reveal about their learning style, interests or areas of need? This step ensures that observations contribute meaningfully to the child's overall development plan.

Incorporating an understanding of each child's learning style, as outlined by Gardner's multiple intelligences theory (Marenus, 2024), further enhances the observation process. Children learn in different ways – some are naturally inclined towards movement (kinaesthetic intelligence), while others might excel in verbal or linguistic tasks. Recognising these preferences helps educators tailor both their observations and interventions. For example, a child with strong spatial intelligence might thrive in activities like building with blocks or solving puzzles, providing valuable insights that wouldn't be captured by a more general observation method. For children who prefer visual learning, documenting their progress through photographs during art activities can highlight their creativity and problem-solving skills. Similarly, for a child with a strong verbal-linguistic intelligence, using running records of their conversations during group discussions can reveal important aspects of their language development.

Discussions within the team

Collaborative discussions within the ECE team are critical for providing holistic, well-rounded support to each child. These discussions allow educators to share observations, strategies and insights with one another, ensuring that the entire team is aligned in its approach to supporting a child's development. By creating an environment where open communication and reflective practice are encouraged, educators can collectively work towards achieving the best outcomes for every child, particularly those with disabilities, developmental delays or neurodivergence.

A powerful approach to team discussions is to regularly add specific children to the agenda during staff meetings or reflective conversations. By bringing a child into the centre of the conversation, educators can discuss different viewpoints and perspectives from individual staff members who have observed the child at various times throughout the day and in different learning environments. This holistic, wrap-around approach ensures that every aspect of the child's development, needs and strengths is considered.

For instance, during a meeting, the team might focus on Sarah, the four-year-old who has not yet begun walking. Each educator brings their unique perspective based on interactions with Sarah throughout the day. One educator might have observed her social strengths during group time, while another noticed challenges she faced during outdoor play. By pooling these different perspectives, the team can collaborate to develop a comprehensive support plan for Sarah. Team members might decide to introduce strategies such as extra support during physical activities or incorporating more problem-solving tasks that play to her cognitive strengths.

Similarly, for children who may exhibit behaviours of concern, like struggles with transitions or emotional regulation, team members can bring their observations to the table. One educator may suggest introducing visual aids or social stories, while another might recommend more structured and predictable sensory breaks. This collaborative discussion allows for a diversity of ideas, ensuring the team develops strategies that reflect the child's needs across different contexts, such as group activities, quiet time or outdoor play.

This process encourages educators to move beyond their individual perspectives and see the child through a collective lens. It allows for a rich exchange of ideas, ensuring that strategies are not siloed but rather integrated across all learning environments. For example, a strategy that works during morning transitions could be refined and applied during lunch or outdoor play based on the input of various team members. These regular reflective conversations are also crucial when implementing strategies recommended by external specialists, such as speech therapists or occupational therapists.

By discussing how these strategies work across different contexts, educators can ensure they are being applied consistently. For example, if a therapist introduces communication tools, the team can reflect on how those tools are being used during different activities, ensuring they are effective and aligned with the child's needs throughout the day. In addition, team discussions foster a culture of continuous learning and professional development. Educators can learn from each other's experiences and knowledge, share successes and offer support during challenges. This kind of reflective practice not only benefits the children but also strengthens the professional growth of the educators themselves. It encourages a mindset where educators are always seeking to improve their practice – not in isolation, but through collaboration and shared learning.

Here are some examples of staff meeting reflective questions:

1. **What strengths have we observed in this child across different parts of the day, and how can we build on these strengths to support their overall development?** This question helps the team focus on the child's abilities and how they can leverage these strengths in various settings.

2. **What challenges or behaviours of concern have we noticed in different environments (indoor, outdoor, group time), and how can we adapt our strategies to better support the child's needs?** This encourages the team to reflect on specific behaviours and think about contextual factors that may influence the child's responses.

3. **Are there any strategies, interventions or approaches that have worked particularly well with this child in one part of the day that could be applied or adapted in other areas?** This prompts the team to share successful strategies and to consider how they can be integrated across different learning environments.

4. **How consistent are we as a team in implementing support strategies, and what steps can we take to ensure the child experiences continuity in their learning and care?** This encourages discussion around consistency and the importance of aligning approaches across team members to create a stable environment for the child.
5. **What additional perspectives or insights can the family or external professionals (for example, therapists) offer, and how can we ensure that their contributions are reflected in our daily practice?** This prompts the team to think about how external input from families or specialists can be incorporated into the daily care and support provided to the child. It also helps identify potential professional development or learning that may be required.

Relationships with families

Building strong, trusting relationships with families is one of the most important aspects of getting to know each child in the ECEC service. Families offer unique insights into a child's personality, preferences, routines and developmental history that are invaluable for educators. When there is a strong partnership between educators and families, children benefit from a consistent and supportive environment that spans both their home and early learning settings. Establishing meaningful relationships with families begins with open and respectful communication.

From the very first interaction, it is essential that educators take the time to get to know the child's family – learning about their culture, values and expectations for their child's learning and development. Inviting families to share their observations about their child at home, such as the child's favourite activities or how they handle transitions, allows educators to better understand the child and personalise their approach. It also signals to families that their role in their child's learning journey is valued and that their insights are integral to how educators approach the child in the learning environment.

However, it is important to know that building relationships with families takes time, and rushing into deeper conversations can feel uncomfortable for both parties if a foundation of trust hasn't been established. If you do not have a strong relationship with a family, any conversation outside of small talk will be hard for them – and for you. Gradually building these connections is key.

It is also important to remember that not all relationships with families will look the same. Some parents might prefer close, daily communication, while others may prefer a more hands-off approach. Respecting these differences is critical in building trust and ensuring that the relationship feels comfortable for both the family and the educator. It's also important to acknowledge that different families may naturally gravitate towards different educators. Some parents may connect more easily with one educator over another due to personality, communication style or cultural similarities. This isn't something to be discouraged but rather a reflection of the strength of a team environment. The beauty of a diverse team is that different members can establish meaningful connections with different families, ensuring that every child's family feels supported.

While fostering these relationships is essential, maintaining professional boundaries is equally important. Crossing boundaries can create complications that undermine the professional relationship between educators and families. For instance, becoming too personally involved – such as connecting with a parent on social media – can lead to uncomfortable situations. Imagine a scenario where an educator becomes Facebook friends with a parent and then sees posts that they consider inappropriate, such as behaviours or comments that may raise concerns about the family's personal life. This can challenge the relationship because the educator may feel conflicted about what they have seen, while the parent may not expect their social media presence to influence their relationship with the educator.

Navigating these challenges requires professionalism and sensitivity. If an educator finds themselves in this situation, it's important to gracefully and professionally back away from the personal relationship while maintaining a professional rapport. For example, the educator might decide to unfollow or mute the parent on social media to avoid future exposure to potentially uncomfortable situations. In extreme cases, it may be necessary to have a professional conversation with the parent to re-establish boundaries. Either way, educators must be mindful of not crossing lines that could blur the distinction between their professional role and personal relationships, as this can lead to misunderstandings and strain the trust they have worked to build. Having policies to prevent blurring of professional boundaries may be useful.

An example of this could be Corey, a four-year-old who frequently exhibits behavioural outbursts and seems to have more energy than is typically required for the activities at hand. Open and respectful communication with his family about his high energy levels and frequent outbursts might require a more gradual approach. Some families may want daily updates, while others might prefer less frequent, focused discussions. Establishing the right type of communication is key to ensuring that Corey's family feels informed and involved in his progress. Respecting the family's preferences on communication style can make them feel more comfortable, helping the relationship grow organically over time.

Intensity/frequency/duration

When observing and understanding children's behaviour, it is crucial to not only focus on what behaviours are occurring but also to consider their intensity, frequency and duration. These three factors provide a deeper and more meaningful context for understanding a child's actions, especially when the behaviours may be challenging or concerning. By paying close attention to these elements, educators can gain insights into whether certain behaviours are part of typical development, a response to environmental factors or indicative of deeper needs that require intervention.

For example, consider Corey, the four-year-old who frequently exhibits behavioural outbursts and seems to have more energy than is typically required for the activities at hand. His energy levels often exceed those of his peers, leading to disruptive outbursts during structured group activities. Understanding Corey's behaviour through the lens of intensity, frequency and duration can provide valuable insight into how to best support him.

Intensity – refers to the strength or degree of a behaviour. In Corey's case, his outbursts vary in intensity – sometimes he simply talks loudly and fidgets, but other times, his behaviour escalates into running around the room, knocking over materials or shouting over others. Understanding the varying intensities of Corey's behaviour helps educators decide when immediate intervention is needed, such as during highly intense outbursts, versus when gentler redirection or calming techniques may suffice. For a child like Corey, whose behaviours can quickly escalate, it is important to observe when his energy is beginning to build so that interventions can be introduced before the behaviour becomes too intense.

Frequency – refers to how often a behaviour occurs. Corey's high energy outbursts are not isolated incidents – they happen multiple times throughout the day, particularly during structured activities that require sitting still or focusing. By tracking the frequency of Corey's behaviours, educators can identify patterns. They might notice that his outbursts are more frequent during transitions from active play to quieter activities or during long periods of sitting, such as group reading time. This information is critical for understanding that Corey may need more frequent movement opportunities or sensory inputs to help him self-regulate throughout the day.

Duration – refers to how long a behaviour lasts. Some of Corey's outbursts may last only a few minutes, while others can extend much longer, disrupting the flow of the class and his ability to engage in the learning environment. For example, during a story time group time, Corey may start fidgeting after just a few minutes, but if his energy isn't redirected, this can escalate into a longer-lasting outburst that disrupts the entire session. Observing the duration of Corey's behaviour is key in deciding how and when to intervene. Shorter outbursts may be managed by providing him with a fidget tool or offering a brief movement break. However, when his outbursts extend for a significant period, this may suggest that he needs more structured interventions, such as a sensory break or a more flexible learning schedule that better accommodates his high energy levels.

By examining the intensity, frequency and duration of Corey's behaviours, educators can develop targeted strategies to better support him. For example, knowing that his behaviours often occur during group activities, the team might decide to introduce more movement breaks or provide Corey with sensory tools to help him regulate his energy while still participating. They could also work on emotional regulation strategies with Corey, such as helping him identify when he's feeling overstimulated and giving him tools to calm down before his behaviour escalates. Additionally, the team might collaborate with Corey's family regarding strategies they use at home, promoting consistency across environments.

Antecedent Behaviour Consequence (ABC) charts are an effective tool for observing and understanding behaviours like Corey's. An ABC chart helps educators break down behaviour into three key elements: the antecedent (what happens before the behaviour), the behaviour itself and the consequence (what happens after the behaviour).

This method can be especially useful when trying to determine the triggers for behaviours that challenge children and the outcomes that may be reinforcing them. For instance, in Corey's case, an ABC chart might reveal that his outbursts frequently occur after a period of sitting still for too long (the antecedent), and the behaviour itself might involve shouting or running around. The consequence may be that Corey is provided the opportunity to calm his body, or that he is redirected to another activity. By mapping out these patterns, educators can better understand the context in which the behaviour occurs and make informed adjustments. For example, they might plan for shorter sitting periods or introduce movement breaks before Corey becomes overstimulated.

Understanding the intensity, frequency and duration of children's behaviours, like Corey's, also enables educators to track progress over time. For instance, if Corey's intense outbursts become less frequent or shorter in duration, this indicates improvement, even if the behaviour hasn't completely disappeared. Tracking these metrics helps educators and families celebrate small milestones and assess whether current strategies are effective. These factors are particularly important for children with disabilities, developmental delays or neurodivergence, as such children may express their needs differently. Without considering the context of their behaviours, educators risk misunderstanding or misinterpreting their actions. For Corey, who may have neurodivergent traits like sensory sensitivities or difficulties with emotional regulation, understanding the intensity, frequency and duration of his behaviours allows educators to provide nuanced, appropriate support that respects his individual needs.

The role of 'evidence'

In ECEC services, gathering evidence is a critical process that allows educators to track and understand each child's development, learning progress and behavioural patterns. This evidence not only informs how educators support and plan for each child's unique needs but also serves as a basis for discussions with families, specialists and the wider team. By collecting and analysing a variety of evidence, educators can ensure that they are providing individualised, responsive care that is grounded in each child's actual experiences and growth. Keeping written records is an essential aspect of this process, allowing educators to reflect on the child's progress over time and have targeted, productive conversations with families.

Gathering evidence is more than just recording what a child is doing; it is about building a comprehensive picture of the child's development over time. Observing, documenting and reflecting on a child's actions allows educators to identify patterns, track developmental milestones and spot areas where additional support may be required. For example, an educator may gather evidence on Corey's frequent outbursts and high energy levels by recording the intensity, frequency and duration of his behaviour across different activities and times of day. This evidence helps educators understand when Corey is most likely to become overstimulated and can guide strategies to manage his energy levels more effectively.

Evidence also serves as a valuable tool for communicating with families. When discussing a child's development, having concrete examples and data points allows for clearer, more objective conversations. Instead of relying solely on personal interpretations or memory, educators can present families with specific evidence of a child's progress or challenges. For instance, Corey's family might appreciate seeing logs of his behaviour that highlight specific times of day or activities where he struggles. This written record offers insight into patterns and provides the foundation for proposing effective strategies to address Corey's needs.

The importance of keeping written records

Keeping written records – such as observations, interpretations, developmental milestone mapping, jottings of interactions, educator discussions and conversations with families – is essential in ECEC services. These records form the backbone of evidence-gathering, ensuring that all aspects of a child's development are tracked, reflected upon and shared among the team. Written documentation also provides a reference point for educators and families when discussing the child's progress or addressing concerns.

Observations are essential for tracking children's behaviours, needs and learning patterns over time. These observations allow educators to document significant moments, identify patterns and plan future learning experiences. For example, documenting Corey's high energy levels during group activities can reveal when his behaviour intensifies and what environmental factors contribute to it, helping the team implement more targeted interventions, such as providing sensory tools or movement breaks.

Gathering evidence also requires educators to *interpret and analyse* what they observe. This reflection is crucial in understanding the deeper meaning behind a child's actions. Instead of simply recording Corey's outbursts, for instance, educators might interpret these behaviours as a response to overstimulation or frustration. This analysis can inform interventions and help educators work with Corey's family to create consistent strategies across settings.

Regularly mapping a child's progress aligned with *developmental milestones* helps educators identify strengths and areas of need. For children with disabilities, developmental delays or neurodivergence, tracking milestones may require a more individualised approach. For example, rather than focusing solely on Corey's physical development, educators might track his emotional regulation and social engagement, ensuring that all aspects of his development are supported holistically.

Quick jottings that capture a child's everyday interactions and behaviours also offer valuable insights. These jottings help educators track moments that may otherwise be forgotten or overlooked but are significant for understanding a child's development. For instance, jotting down how Corey interacts with peers during playtime can provide insights into his social development and identify areas where support is needed.

Documenting team discussions and reflective conversations ensures that all educators are aligned in their approach to supporting a child. Different educators may observe the child in different contexts, offering diverse perspectives. For example, Corey's energy levels might be represented differently during outdoor play versus group time, and discussing these variations helps the team develop a consistent strategy across the day. Writing down the outcomes of these discussions creates accountability and consistency across the team.

Written records also play a key role in *family engagement*. Having documented observations and evidence makes it easier to have targeted, objective conversations with families about their child's development. For instance, instead of simply telling Corey's parents that he struggles during group time, educators can share specific written observations and discuss what strategies have been effective in supporting him. This not only builds trust but also ensures that families feel involved and informed in their child's learning journey.

In Chapter 3, we will expand on the role of written records in guiding conversations with families, highlighting how maintaining detailed documentation is essential for having open, supportive and solution-oriented discussions.

The purpose of gathering evidence is to inform decision-making about how best to support each child. Written records provide a detailed, objective view of the child's progress, helping educators tailor their approach and adjust strategies as needed. For example, in Corey's case, the evidence gathered from written observations and team discussions might indicate that providing regular sensory breaks helps support his energy levels, leading to fewer outbursts. Educators can track whether this strategy reduces the intensity and frequency of his behaviours, ensuring they are offering the most effective support.

Key takeaways

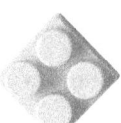

- Taking the time to build positive relationships with children and families is essential for all educators.
- Having trusting and honest relationships with colleagues will ensure that conversations about children and families are respectful and serve a specific purpose.
- Educators need a strong understanding of child development.

- Observations are essential for all educators to understand the children they work with.
- Transition into the ECEC service is an important move and can lay the foundation for inclusion.

Reflective questions for professional learning

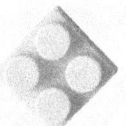

- How effectively do we track the intensity, frequency and duration of children's behaviours in our observations, and how do these insights inform our tailored responses and interventions?
- Are we utilising a diverse range of observation methods to capture a holistic view of each child, especially those with disabilities, developmental delays or neurodivergence?
- How do we ensure that our analysis and interpretation of observations go beyond surface-level behaviours, and how do we link these to developmental milestones and learning goals for each child?
- How can we better incorporate family input and perspectives into our observations and evidence-gathering practices, ensuring that our communication with families is based on concrete, documented information?
- How do we use our team discussions and reflective conversations to consistently share insights and strategies for supporting children, and what can we do to improve collaboration in understanding each child's needs?
- What steps do we take to maintain clear professional boundaries with families, and how do we address situations where boundaries have been crossed, such as through social media interactions or personal relationships?

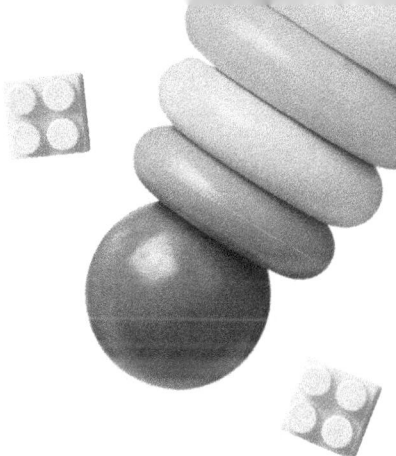

Chapter 3

Having targeted conversations with families

Inclusion of children with disabilities, developmental delays or neurodivergence should never be seen as optional. As we have previously indicated, educators should always place children's rights at the centre of all decisions. One child does not have more rights than another – which is clearly stated in the UNCRC. Remember the quote in Chapter 1? "All children have all these rights, no matter who they are, where they live, what language they speak, what their religion is, what they think, what they look like, if they are a boy or girl, if they have a disability, if they are rich or poor, and no matter who their parents or families are or what their parents or families believe or do. No child should be treated unfairly for any reason" (United Nations, 1989).

So, what does this mean for early childhood educators?

There are many different scenarios that you may encounter, which will result in different approaches.

- Children may enrol in your service with diagnosed disabilities they may have had since birth or for some time.
- Parents may have had thoughts that their child is having difficulty meeting developmental milestones which they raise with you, or they confirm when you approach them.

- Parents have no idea their child may have disabilities, developmental delays or neurodivergence, and when you raise this, they may or may not agree.

When a child comes to the service with a diagnosis, their family may have already had time to adjust emotionally to living with disabilities and developed an understanding of how to support their child's specific learning needs; and may also be knowledgeable about the National Disability Insurance Scheme early childhood approach and have support for both their child and themselves. This provides a great foundation for you to work collaboratively in understanding the child and setting meaningful and relevant goals.

If you are questioning whether a child requires additional support and you speak with a parent who welcomes your perspective, this is also an easier path for educators. You may actually be validating concerns a parent has expressed, and they may be really reassured by the extra support you can offer. You can gain a really good understanding of what they see as the priorities for their child. You can also offer support in helping refer them towards diagnosis if that is what they want, and to additional services that their child may benefit from.

The focus of this chapter, however, is on the situations where parents have no idea their child may have disabilities, developmental delays or neurodivergence which they may or may not agree with. This can be a situation that is difficult for both educators and parents, so learning more about navigating this can provide reassurance to everyone.

Consider Nate, a three-year-old child who has been in your service for about two months, attending two days a week. He does not seem to engage with the educators or the children, but instead seems to wander from one area in the service to another. He does not use words to communicate and seems to find it hard to follow instructions. Nate often has toileting accidents; although he will wee on the toilet when you take him, he does not go in on his own, or when other children are going. His mum had indicated that he was still learning to use the toilet when Nate enrolled.

When you have watched Nate playing, he does not really engage in any functional play; for example, if he picks up a car, instead of driving it on the ground, he looks closely at it and spins the wheels. On another occasion, you notice him next to the Play-Doh table and he stands next to it instead of sitting down, and just taps the rolling pin repeatedly on the table.

These examples are things that happen each day. Nate does seem to like being on the swing and will sit there for extended periods of time just swinging back and forth. During any small group times, Nate gets up and wanders away. While he does not distract other children, he will just take himself away from the group and go and get a car and spin the wheels. Nate sits with the other children at morning tea and lunchtime, but he does not engage in any of the conversation or express any emotions such as laughing with other children.

Other educators in the service have shared similar observations with you. You decide to review some of the milestones for a three-year-old. Based on your knowledge of child development, you decide to look at the two- to three-year ones, as you are aware of both social and language behaviours that are not reflecting your understanding of preschoolers' development. The EYLF developmental milestones identify criteria that might suggest additional advice is needed. The following are the ones you have identified from that list:

Seek advice if a child is not:

- Interested in playing
- Understanding simple instructions
- Using many words
- Joining words in meaningful phrases
- Interested in others.

(ACECQA, 2018a)

While you recognise that Nate has only been in the service for a short time, you feel your observations have provided enough information to you to identify that Nate may require some extra support. You could choose to 'wait and see', but research indicates that early intervention is the best approach (Healthy Trajectories, 2022). As you have already spoken to other educators who share your perspective, it is important to set up a conversation with Nate's parent/s to find out what they have noticed regarding his strengths, interests and any areas they believe he might need additional support.

Being prepared for a targeted conversation with a parent/s

When educators are the first to identify concerns with a child's development, it can be very confronting for these educators to have a conversation with the family. First, think about which educator the parent/s feel the most comfortable with. Can they be part of this meeting with the parent/s? You want to avoid appearing like you are a 'panel' that parents need to address, so make sure there are not more than two educators. If, for example, a trainee in the service has a really great relationship with Nate's mum but does not feel confident to have this targeted conversation with her, the trainee may work with the director or educational leader to have this conversation together.

Being prepared by working out who will say what, how the conversation will evolve and what the role of each person is will ensure the conversation is supportive, professional and achieves the goal of helping Nate's parent/s share their thoughts and understand the service perspective. Sometimes these conversations can become emotional, so being prepared will help achieve the best outcomes.

Some parents may be overwhelmed by this conversation, and their reaction can be unpredictable. Educators need to be prepared for these conversations and for a range of responses from parents.

How can you be prepared for these conversations?

- Set up a time with the parent/s that is convenient to them and so that it will not be rushed.
- Ensure there is a comfortable space in the service where you can meet without disruption or distraction.
- Have your written observations with you, as well as some key developmental milestone information.
- It might be useful to have some information about local support services that may be beneficial for either Nate or the parent/s – such as supported playgroup, paediatrician or speech therapist, to name a few.

During the meeting

There are a number of things you can do to make the meeting more positive for everyone. During the meeting, consider doing the following:

- Offer a cup of coffee or a glass of water to help the parent/s feel settled. As they have only been in the service for a short time, it is important to build a rapport.
- Explain that you have asked them to come in as you have noticed some things that Nate is doing that you would like to discuss.
- Ask them what they have noticed about Nate's language and social interactions.
- Ask if they have any other concerns about Nate's behaviour or development, and if they have had any discussion or follow-up from any health professional about these concerns.
- Go through some of your written observations, so you can share why you think there may be some developmental differences.
- Remind them that developmental difference is just that. All children are different, and milestones are just a guide. It is about identifying any areas where Nate would benefit from extra support, helping them recognise that the first five years is the most sensitive period for a child's development.

- Acknowledge how difficult this conversation can be, but reassure them the goal is to look at how you can all work together to progress Nate's development.

A range of parent reactions

As previously identified, you may be the first person to raise this with a child's parent/s, which can result in a wide range of reactions. Everyone is different, and there may be a reaction that does not align with those identified here. However, this will hopefully give you a starting point to work from.

If the parent has been noticing that other children (either their own or others) seem to be using a lot of verbal language at three years of age, they may have been wondering why Nate is not. They may have noticed other children of a similar age playing with each other, or engaging in some pretend play, or functional play (where toys are used for their purpose – such as driving a car along the ground and making *vroom-vroom* sounds). On some occasions they may have even discussed this with others (either another parent or grandparent) who has 'brushed them off'.

When you raise this with the parent/s, they identify some of the things they have noticed, and you can then agree that you have also noticed those same things. By showing them some of the things that research tells us most children will do within age ranges can be really validating for them and reassure them they are not imagining things. This is a great foundation, as there is already a shared understanding from which your discussions and ideas can be built.

You may, however, find Nate's parent/s may have no idea that Nate might be having some difficulties with communication and social interaction, but are very welcoming of your observations, which will alert them to start focusing on Nate in different situations so a more comprehensive picture can be built. Again, this provides a shared foundation.

On other occasions, parents can seem to be very defensive and almost abrasive in the way they respond when you raise differences you have observed. If Nate's parent/s do not agree with you, and say that he speaks when he is at home and has no problem playing with other children outside the service, there are a couple of reasons for this:

1. It is possible that Nate is just quietly settling into the service, and once he becomes more relaxed and comfortable in this environment, his communication and social interaction will increase.
2. Nate may experience communication difficulties and limited social interest and interaction with others, but his parent/s are either not aware of this, or are not ready to consider that he may have disabilities, developmental delays or be neurodivergent. Remember, this can be really difficult news for parents to receive, so be mindful of your reaction. You can reassure them that you will continue to observe and ask that they do the same, then maybe you can meet again in a month or so to share your observations. You may decide to share an observation template or explain some of the things they could look out for if you feel that is helpful.

Assuming you know their child better than parents do when you have observed for only two days a week for two months is inappropriate and can come across as intimidating. It can also be that a parent is really scared of what the differences they have seen in their child might mean. This may be because any sort of disabilities, developmental delays or neurodivergence they have experienced comes from a stereotyped image in the media. There are lots of reasons for different reactions, so don't judge parents for their response.

After the meeting

Remember that the majority of parents are wanting what is best for their children, so their reluctance to go along with your perspective is not because they don't want to help. They may genuinely not have noticed, or they may not be emotionally ready to consider any developmental difference. Your role is to continue to build a trusting relationship with Nate's parents, share his interests and strengths, and don't just focus on things you feel he needs support with. While these are important, sometimes parents might start to feel uncomfortable with you because of your constant and persistent approach about areas of concern to you. These are just part of Nate's overall development, so just focus on the relationship you are building with the family and share any strategies you feel are supporting Nate in the service.

You need to continue observing Nate and gathering information about his interests, strengths, ways he seems to respond best, communication strategies he is using as well as any things he seems to need support with. Be sure to record all of this information, so you can share it with his parent/s. During drop-off and pick-up times, continue to share information about Nate – but remember to communicate all the positive things you see. This does not mean you should not share the things you feel Nate needs support with. Imagine if Nate's parent/s are feeling overwhelmed from your initial meeting, then you constantly share your concerns. The parents may feel the easiest option is to withdraw him from your service, or they may choose to try to avoid you when they do come into the service.

Both of these options are unacceptable. The principles within the EYLF include both building secure, respectful and reciprocal relationships; and partnerships (AGDE, 2022, p.11). Not only are these essential, but the overall focus on Belonging, Being and Becoming are also crucial. It is not enough for children to feel a sense of belonging, but families also need to feel they belong to the service. Ultimately, developing a respectful and collaborative relationship with Nate's parent/s will bring about the most positive outcomes for Nate (Reimagine Australia, 2024).

Strength-based terminology

While it is crucial to share concerns with parents, strength-based terminology will help them realise you are seeing their whole child, not just a developmental difference. All children have strengths and interests, so be sure to also share your observations of things Nate is enjoying and things you have seen as strengths.

It is also important to remember that it is not the role of educators to diagnose children. They are well placed to identify developmental differences, but not qualified to diagnose any disabilities or neurodivergence. Using diagnostic terminology is inappropriate and can cause parents confusion and additional stress. Sometimes your previous experience might lead you to suspect a particular diagnosis, but this is something that a medical or allied health practitioner is responsible for, for example, a psychologist, speech therapist or paediatrician. Educators need to identify information that reflects the strengths and the developmental differences you have seen, really using a critical lens to think about the context, environment, strategies educators are using, and not just what Nate is doing in isolation.

When speaking with parents or anyone else, it is also necessary to remember that language needs to be positive and affirming. Using language that is negative or limiting leads to a social perception that difference is less. Diversity is what makes our world, and developmental difference is just one area of diversity. Every individual should be valued and celebrated for who they are.

Why do you need evidence of your concerns?

If you decide to have a conversation with Nate's parents and you do not have any observations written down, it can be seen as quite speculative and unprofessional. As these conversations may be overwhelming for the educators, too, not having anything written can mean they either forget things they want to mention, or they go off on tangents that might be confusing for everyone. You have hopefully seen a wide range of situations, behaviours, actions and responses across the past two months since Nate began, which have led to you feeling Nate is demonstrating some developmental difference. There is no way you can remember all that information with accuracy without it being recorded.

Imagine instead that you have recorded 30 different observations that you have interpreted or analysed to really build your understanding of Nate. You would have then seen things Nate is enjoying, areas he may be finding challenging, and also why you are wanting to follow up with his parent/s. However, presenting parents with a pile of written observations can also be overwhelming. Consider the unique needs, culture and perspectives of an individual family to ensure the way information is delivered is appropriate for them.

Having a knowledge of developmental milestones is important. While they are not a definitive list that should be used as a pass/fail checklist, they can provide you with important guidelines. They are designed to help recognise age ranges when the majority of children will achieve particular skills. They are not designed to make people feel bad about what a child is not doing, but instead, a guideline to help understand where a child may need some additional support.

If you have recorded observations and some milestone information to share with Nate's parent/s, you can then refer to these factual documents rather than being caught up in an emotion or confusion that results within the conversation. Having this written information also means you can give it to Nate's parent/s to take home, so they can spend some more time looking over it if they want to.

This might seem a bit black and white and scare some families off, so again, be sure to consider the culture, needs and perspectives of each family. Remember that the relationships developed with families and connections made are crucial.

Shared understanding

In an ECEC service, there are multiple educators who all engage in conversations with families during the drop-off and pick-up of children. It is hoped that all educators would be having friendly conversations with Nate's parent/s, but it is important to respectfully discuss the approach you are taking to having a targeted conversation, who will be involved, and if any future enquiries are made by Nate's parent/s, whether they should be directed to a specific person.

This will ensure that all information going to Nate's family is consistent and responsive to the current situation. For example, if Nate's parent/s do not believe there are any areas of development that might need additional support, it is important that your whole staff is aware of this, and what the next steps will be. If someone is not aware of this and they engage in a conversation making an assumption about how Nate's parent/s might react, this could potentially confuse his parent/s or reduce their confidence in the service as a whole.

What is really important is that the shared discussion between educators (and potentially other staff such as kitchen or office staff) is not judgemental, but rather a respectful dialogue to ensure everyone understands the current situation. This is also important as you will need to share specific strategies you are all going to adopt to assist Nate's learning. In addition, everyone needs to share a commitment to the philosophy of the service, the rights of all children and the principles of inclusion.

Key takeaways

- Educators need to ensure they have a comprehensive understanding of child development to recognise when children require additional support.
- Remember to get to know every child – their strengths, interests, likes, dislikes and any areas requiring additional support. Observation is essential!
- It is important that disabilities, developmental delays and neurodivergence are not viewed as deficits – rather, just unique qualities of an individual child.
- Targeted conversations are important, and it is necessary to share your views with families when you feel a child may need additional support.
- It is not acceptable to care for a particular child without offering educational opportunities relevant to them. ECEC encompasses both education and care for all children.
- Targeted conversations can be hard – for both educators and parents. Preparation is key!
- If parents demonstrate distress in their verbal responses or within their body language, validation and empathy is critical to reduce distress and enable regulation to support optimal communication between both parties.
- Be prepared for a targeted conversation with a parent. Having written information ensures you can share specific examples with parents, but it also means you can stay focused on the purpose of the meeting.
- Remember to acknowledge that parents have different views, and that is OK!
- Educators need to have respectful and professional shared conversations to ensure everyone understands not only individual children, but families and the engagement that others are having with them.

- Remember that families know their child best, and they have the most powerful influence on their child's development.
- Working with families is crucial to success.

Reflective questions for professional learning

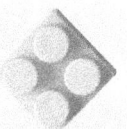

- If you noticed a child was having some difficulties engaging in social interaction with other children and educators, what are some of the things you could do?
- If a targeted conversation with a parent was needed, who would conduct it?
- What are some of the locations in the service that may be appropriate to use for a targeted conversation?
- Following a targeted conversation, what is the process to ensure all staff members understand what has been discussed and what the current focus will be?
- If a parent/family is indicating signs of distress during a targeted conversation, what are some practical ways you might respond to reduce distress?

Chapter 4

A collaborative, integrated approach

This chapter explores the importance of an integrated, collaborative approach to early intervention. Chapter 1 introduced the concept of early intervention, and we will explore this further, including different professionals who are involved within a child's team.

Collaboration in early intervention

For early intervention to be most effective, it is important to adopt a collaborative approach, where everyone is working in the best interests of the child and their family.

Understanding the importance of collaboration

In ECEC services, collaboration is essential – with children, with families and with colleagues. The EYLF V2.0 identifies collaboration as, "working together cooperatively towards common goals. Collaboration is achieved through information sharing, joint planning and the development of common understandings and objectives" (AGDE, 2022, p.65).

While collaboration is important across many aspects of an ECEC service, it plays a critical role in ensuring effective and comprehensive supports for children with disabilities, developmental delays or neurodivergence. Not only do educators need to collaborate with children, families and colleagues within the service, it is also the educators' responsibility to collaborate within the child's care team.

What do we mean by a child's 'care team'? Every child has a circle of professionals, loved ones and carers to support their learning, development and play. For instance, a child may have their parents, grandparents, soccer coach, general practitioner, paediatrician and their early childhood educators. Another child in your room may have their parents, grandparents, early childhood educators, paediatrician, speech pathologist, physiotherapist and art teacher. These are examples of a child's care team – the adults and support people within the child's life. We can think of Bronfenbrenner's ecological model, where the care team is made up of the people who would feature in the child's microsystem.

Figure 4: Bronfenbrenner's Ecological Systems Theory

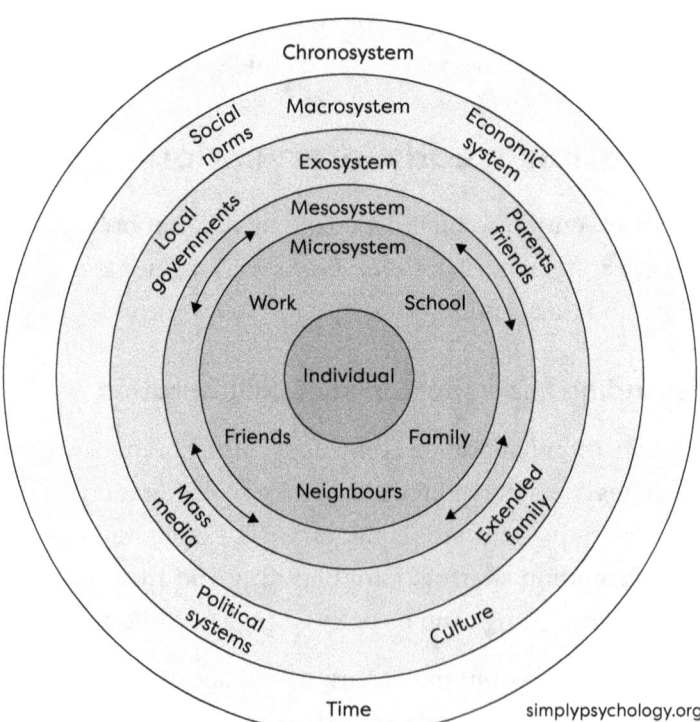

Combining expertise from various disciplines and experiences creates a cohesive support system that maximises each child's developmental trajectory and learning opportunities. Ideally, educators, therapists and families will work together, share information and strategies, and develop goals to provide a holistic approach. The synergy created through collaborative practices leads to more informed decision-making, consistent implementation of strategies across different environments and a shared understanding of the child's progress.

This chapter will delve into the importance of collaboration in early intervention, providing best practices and practical steps to implement collaborative approaches within ECEC services. Through this integrated approach, we aim to empower educators and families to work together seamlessly, creating the best possible outcomes for children in their service.

In Australia, only about 50% of one-year-olds and 35% of children aged between one and four years access maternal child health nursing services (Garg et al., 2018). The Australian Government recommends ongoing developmental screening during health checks at six, 12 and 18 months, and at two, three and four years of age (Royal Australian College of General Practitioners, 2018). As early childhood educators, it is crucial to understand the importance of developmental screening, assessment and monitoring in our settings. These words can be used separately and interchangeably depending on the context of the setting and the professionals involved. For the purpose of this text, we will be using the term 'developmental screening'.

Developmental screening involves using specific tools to identify areas of development in children who may have certain developmental delays. It's important to note that screening is not diagnostic, but serves as an early identification tool (Mozolic-Staunton et al., 2020). This proactive measure allows us to identify potential developmental concerns early on, paving the way for timely supports (intervention).

In 2016, Reimagine Australia, formerly known as Early Childhood Intervention Australia, published the *National Guidelines for Best Practice in Early Childhood Intervention*, focusing on core quality areas aimed at enhancing outcomes for children and families. As early childhood educators, it is crucial for us to recognise the significance of these guidelines as they form the fundamental basis for collaboration within a child's entire care team. Genuine early childhood support (intervention) involves embracing family-centred and strength-based practices, which acknowledge the central role of families and fosters collaboration between educators and allied health professionals in planning interventions.

This approach not only respects the unique perspectives and priorities of each family, but it also creates a sense of empowerment and ownership in the decision-making process regarding their child's development. Furthermore, by leveraging family strengths and resources, educators can create a more inclusive and supportive environment that meets the diverse needs of children and families. The integration of evidence-based standards, accountability and practice serves as a crucial complement to the family-centred and strength-based approach in collaborative practice. It stands as a basis in ensuring that intervention and support strategies are firmly grounded in the latest research findings and clinical expertise. This commitment to evidence-based practice empowers educators to stay abreast of emerging evidence and best practices, enabling them to continually refine their approaches to better address the diverse needs of children (Reimagine Australia, 2016).

Steps to implementing collaboration

Integrated collaboration in early childhood intervention entails a comprehensive and structured approach aimed at fostering seamless coordination among educators, allied health professionals and families. The care team should ensure there are appropriate and effective platforms for collaborative communication. This could be as simple as a group email thread, a shared digital document or a digital collaboration platform. The tool or digital platform should be easily accessible for the family to use and have access to. We need to take into consideration the families' communication preferences and needs (verbal, text, pictures, etc.). It is best to utilise the communication method that the family prefers to use, although using several forms of communication is recommended, as everyone in the care team may not always communicate through the one pathway.

Alongside the communication pathways, establishing regular care team meetings is essential for bringing the team members together to connect, communicate and collaborate effectively. These meetings serve as valuable opportunities for stakeholders to convene, exchange insights and align strategies to best support the child's intervention. Typically held every three to six months, with the frequency adjusted based on the family's needs and the addition of new team members, these meetings are pivotal in promoting a holistic approach to intervention.

During these sessions, maintaining open and honest communication channels among all parties is imperative. As an educator, you may feel hesitant about sharing observations with the child's care team, but this is important as long as parents have given permission to do so. Educators often observe the child in a unique environment, where their behaviours and responses may differ from other settings. Factors such as the child's comfort level in a larger group, exposure to various communication styles among educators, and differing learning and sensory experiences between home and ECEC services can significantly impact their development.

Steps to goal setting

The concept of goal setting may appear straightforward at first glance. It involves crafting goals aligned with the EYLF to ensure comprehensive support across various developmental outcomes. You may be familiar with the SMART goal approach, where goals are:

- Specific
- Measurable
- Achievable
- Relevant
- Time-bound.

These SMART goals serve as guiding principles, providing clarity and enabling monitoring of progress, often documented through observations and integrated into the service's planning cycle. However, in practice, we have observed instances where SMART goals are misaligned or persistently extended from short- to long-term objectives throughout a child's time in the service.

Educators should establish a person-centred approach that leads to growing recognition that children should be actively involved in their own goal setting. Evidence-based teaching strategies support goal setting to enhance collaborative practice, and direct planning of early childhood supports (intervention) towards meaningful areas for children and their families (Kuper et al., 2014). Research findings indicate that child-led goal setting has the potential to positively influence the child-educator relationship, engagement in the learning environment, development of self-determination skills, and outcomes. However, children with disabilities, developmental delays or neurodivergence currently have a marginal role in goal setting compared to their care team (Curtis et al., 2021). Their goals are usually tailored to managing their behaviour, safety or compliance within the daily routine of the service. Effective goal setting for a child with disabilities, developmental delays or neurodivergence should be at the forefront of collaboration within the child's care team.

A contemporary approach to goal setting across the education sector is the concept of neuro-affirming goal setting.

Neurodiversity – is a concept that acknowledges the natural variations in human brain functioning, thinking and processing. It acknowledges that neurological differences, such as autism spectrum disorder (ASD), attention deficit hyperactivity disorder (ADHD), dyslexia and other cognitive variations are not deficits or disorders, but rather part of the broad spectrum of human diversity. The neurodiversity movement advocates for the acceptance and inclusion of individuals with these differences, promoting the idea that these variations contribute to the richness of human experience and should be valued and supported within society.

Neuro-affirming practice – is an approach that seeks to create environments, practices and attitudes that support and celebrate neurodivergent individuals in a way that honours their unique perspectives and experiences. Rather than trying to make neurodivergent people conform to neurotypical standards, a neuro-affirming approach focuses on understanding and addressing their specific needs, fostering their strengths and providing support that empowers them to thrive. This approach encourages the importance of creating inclusive and respectful spaces where neurodivergent individuals are valued for who they are, with their voices and choices at the centre of their care and support.

Neuro-affirming goals – are designed with the understanding that neurodiversity is a natural and valuable part of human diversity, and they aim to support the unique ways neurodivergent individuals process information, interact with their environment and communicate. Rather than focusing on changing or 'fixing' a child's behaviour to conform to neurotypical standards, neuro-affirming goals focus on enhancing the individual's strengths, respecting their needs, and fostering environments that are supportive and inclusive. These goals prioritise the child's perspective, ensuring that their voice is central in the development process. They also consider the importance of consistency, predictability and secure relationships, recognising that these factors are crucial for the child's emotional and social wellbeing.

Application in different settings

Educators in ECEC services play a multifaceted role, not only delivering an early childhood curriculum, but also facilitating care, social-emotional development, fostering creativity, physical development, language and communication, and promoting critical thinking skills. By focusing on developmental milestones, educators ensure that interventions are tailored to meet the unique needs and abilities of each child, fostering a supportive and enriching learning environment.

As an educator, your role transcends traditional teaching. It encompasses nurturing every aspect of a child's developmental journey. This multifaceted role involves delivering education outcomes, but it also requires you to foster developmental milestones, stages and goals.

At home, parents and caregivers usually have their child's best interests at the forefront, and often focus on functional development and life skills. They also play a pivotal role in reinforcing skills acquired in ECEC services by integrating supportive activities into daily routines. The home environment offers valuable opportunities for children to practise and apply skills learned in ECEC services, promoting continuity in learning experiences.

Parents can support their child's development by engaging in activities that reinforce concepts, strategies and outcomes taught in the ECEC service. These activities not only reinforce learning outcomes but also strengthen the parent-child bond. The goal is to create a seamless transition between learning environments, ensuring that skills acquired in the education setting are continually reinforced at home and vice versa.

Similarly, in therapy sessions, therapeutic goals are coordinated with those established in ECEC services and home environments, ensuring a cohesive and integrated approach to supporting the child's development. Collaboration among educators, therapists and other care team members is essential to ensure that interventions are coordinated and consistent across different settings. By aligning therapeutic goals with those established in other environments, therapists can reinforce and build upon the progress made in ECEC services and at home.

Consistent implementation across settings

Consistency in ECEC services, home and therapy environments plays a crucial role in supporting the overall development of children, particularly those with disabilities, developmental delays or neurodivergence. At its core, consistency means keeping things the same across different settings where a child spends time. This could involve using the same routines, rules, expectations and ways of communicating so that the child experiences a similar approach everywhere they go. Children thrive when they know what to expect.

There are many benefits to being consistent across a child's natural settings. These can include:

- Building a secure and predictable environment
- Reinforcing learning, expectations and behaviour
- Reducing stress and anxiety
- Enhancing communication and collaboration
- Building trust and emotional and relational safety.

Creating a secure and predictable environment is foundational for the healthy development of children, particularly in their early years. This concept is rooted in the understanding that children flourish in environments where they feel safe, understand what to expect and can anticipate the outcomes of their actions. Such an environment not only supports emotional wellbeing but also plays a critical role in holistic development.

Predictability in a child's environment refers to the consistency of routines, expectations and responses from caregivers and educators. Regularity in daily activities – such as consistent times for meals, play and rest – provides children with a sense of stability. This stability is essential as it offers structure within which children can explore, learn and play. For instance, when a child understands the sequence of daily living events, such as knowing that playtime is followed by a snack and then story time, they develop a clearer sense of how their day is organised. This understanding enhances their ability to feel in control of their environment, reducing anxiety and promoting a sense of security.

The concept of security extends beyond physical safety to encompass emotional security, where children feel valued and supported by the adults in their lives. Emotional security is a critical component of development, as it encourages children to take developmental risks, such as attempting new tasks or expressing their thoughts and feelings. This willingness to take risks is vital for fostering resilience, problem-solving abilities and independence.

Furthermore, emotional security enables children to form healthy relationships, as they learn to trust and rely on the consistent presence and support of their caregivers and educators. The role of caregivers and educators in establishing a secure and predictable environment is paramount. These individuals are responsible for setting the tone and structure of the child's daily experiences. By maintaining a calm, patient and consistent approach, caregivers and educators help children understand what is expected of them and how they can meet those expectations. For example, a child who consistently receives positive reinforcement from their early childhood educator for using kind words or helping with tidying up the play area is more likely to continue engaging in those behaviours. In contrast, unpredictable responses from educators – such as inconsistently acknowledging or overlooking these actions – can lead to confusion and anxiety in the child, undermining their ability to understand and follow social norms within the learning environment.

Moreover, a predictable environment fosters the confidence children need to explore their surroundings and engage in new experiences. Such exploration is crucial for cognitive development, as it stimulates curiosity, experimentation and hypothesising. When children feel secure in their environment, they are more likely to engage in activities that challenge their abilities, thereby facilitating the development of new skills and knowledge. For example, a child who feels safe and supported is more inclined to attempt building a complex structure with blocks, even if the outcome is uncertain. This willingness to engage with new challenges is a significant driver of cognitive and creative development.

Focusing on reducing stress and anxiety in children is crucial, as it directly enhances their emotional and relational safety – a goal that is best achieved through solid consistency in both the physical and relational environments they encounter daily. A consistent and stable environment plays a critical role in mitigating feelings of uncertainty and apprehension that children may experience. When children are exposed to consistent routines and clear expectations, they are less likely to feel overwhelmed or anxious. The predictability of their daily lives offers a comforting sense of security and control, which is essential in alleviating the uncertainty that often triggers anxiety. Knowing what to expect, whether at home, in the early learning environment or during therapy sessions, helps children anticipate the flow of their day, providing them with a reassuring sense of expectations and routine.

The predictability of a child's environment is intrinsically linked to their perception of the adults who care for them. When caregivers, educators and therapists respond in consistent and supportive ways, children begin to develop a deep-seated trust that their needs will be met reliably. This trust forms the cornerstone of emotional safety, as it instils in children the confidence that they are in a secure environment where they are understood, valued and supported. Emotional safety transcends the mere physical aspect of security; it encompasses the assurance that children will receive emotional support, that their feelings will be acknowledged and validated, and that they will be guided through challenging situations with compassion and empathy.

Relational safety is another vital component that develops in tandem with emotional safety. When children feel secure in their relationships with the adults in their lives, they are more likely to form strong, positive bonds. These relationships become a cornerstone of comfort and stability, further reducing stress and anxiety.

The consistent, positive interactions children have with their caregivers and educators help them build a foundation of trust, which is essential for healthy emotional and social development. Trusting relationships provide children with the reassurance that they are not alone, that they have a dependable support system to turn to in times of need.

Understanding Individual Education Plans

Inclusion Support Plans (ISPs), Individual Education Plans and Individual Learning Plans (ILPs) are terms that may sound different, but they fundamentally serve the same purpose: ensuring that every child – particularly those with diverse needs – receives the support necessary to fully participate in their educational environment and strive toward their potential. While the terminology might vary depending on the context or learning environment, each of these plans shares a common goal – to tailor educational experiences to meet the unique needs of individual children. For this text, we will be using the term Individual Education Plans (IEPs). Their primary focus is to remove barriers to learning, provide targeted support, differentiate teaching strategies and promote an inclusive environment where all children can realise their potential.

An IEP is a comprehensive and individualised framework that serves as a cornerstone in ensuring that children with diverse needs can fully participate and succeed in their learning environment. These plans are essential tools to create inclusive educational settings where every child, regardless of their abilities, challenges or backgrounds, is given the same educational opportunities. The core of any IEP is its individualised approach. These plans recognise that each child is unique, with distinct strengths, challenges and learning styles.

A one-size-fits-all approach to education simply doesn't work for all children, particularly those with disabilities, developmental delays or neurodivergence. An IEP is developed based on a thorough assessment of the child's current abilities, needs and potential. Ideally, this assessment is usually carried out by a multidisciplinary team that includes the child's key educators, therapists, such as speech pathologist or psychologists, and the child's family (care team). The collaborative nature of these plans ensures that they are holistic, considering not only academic needs but also cognitive, social, emotional, language and physical development.

One of the critical aspects of IEPs is their flexibility and responsiveness. Children's needs can change over time, and it is crucial that the plans are regularly reviewed and updated to reflect these changes. This ensures that the support provided remains relevant and effective. The goals set within these plans are typically specific, measurable, achievable, relevant and time-bound (SMART), allowing for clear tracking of the child's progress. Regular reviews also provide an opportunity for all stakeholders – including the child, their family, educators and therapy team to reflect on what is working well and what might need adjustment.

Moreover, IEPs play a critical role in promoting equity in education. They help to 'level the playing field' by providing children with the support they need to overcome barriers to learning and participation. This is particularly important in educational systems that are often designed with the assumption that all students will progress in the same way and at the same pace. ISPs, IEPs and ILPs challenge this assumption by recognising that diversity in learning is not only normal but should be embraced and supported.

The implementation of IEPs also fosters a culture of collaboration and communication among educators, families and allied health professionals. This collaboration is essential for the success of the plans, as it ensures that everyone involved is working towards the same goals and using consistent strategies. It also helps to create a shared understanding of the child's needs and progress, which can be particularly empowering for families. When parents and caregivers feel that they are active partners in their child's education, they are more likely to feel supported and involved, which in turn positively impacts the child's experience.

IEPs are essential in promoting educational equity by providing tailored support to children, helping them overcome barriers to learning and participation. Educational equity refers to the practice of ensuring that every student has access to the resources, opportunities and support they need to succeed, regardless of their background, abilities or challenges. Unlike equality, which treats all students the same, educational equity distinguishes that different children have different needs, and that some may require additional support to achieve success.

Through the implementation of IEPs, educators play a crucial role in fostering educational equity within their learning environments. These plans challenge the traditional assumption that all children progress and learn at the same rate and in the same way, embracing the diversity of learning styles and needs as strengths to be supported. Regularly tracking changes and outcomes, and making reasonable and necessary adjustments based on the plan's guidance allows educators and the child's care team to collaboratively support the child's growth, development and learning.

Furthermore, IEPs empower stakeholders to advocate for additional resources or supports as needed. This advocacy is a critical component of educational equity, as it ensures that children are not just placed in inclusive settings, but that they are genuinely supported in ways that meet their specific needs. The collaborative process involved in creating and maintaining IEPs brings together all stakeholders, ensuring that everyone is aligned and working towards common goals with consistent strategies. This collaboration not only enhances the effectiveness of the IEPs but also empowers families by involving them as active partners in their child's education, leading to a more inclusive and supportive learning environment for the child.

Case study: Implementing inclusive practices at an ECEC service

Background

A community-based ECEC service supports a diverse group of children, including children with various disabilities, development delays or neurodivergence. The service's philosophy focuses on the importance of inclusivity, ensuring that all children, regardless of their abilities or challenges, can fully participate in the learning environment. Recently, the educators at the service identified a need to enhance their approach to managing challenging behaviours and supporting children with sensory processing difficulties. To address these needs, the service decided to implement a range of inclusive practices designed to foster positive engagement and create a more supportive learning environment.

Challenges

One of the key challenges faced by the educators was the need to support Sam, a four-year-old child diagnosed with ASD level 3 and sensory processing difficulties. Sam seemed to find transitions between activities a challenge, often leading to frustration and aggressive behaviours, such as hitting or pushing peers. Additionally, Sam struggled to engage in group activities, frequently isolating himself due to sensory overload. The educators recognised that they needed to create a more structured and predictable environment to help Sam feel secure and reduce his anxiety.

Goals within the IEP

Goal 1: **Support sensory regulation**

Objective: For Sam to use designated sensory tools, such as noise-cancelling headphones or fidget items, to self-regulate during transitions or in potentially overstimulating environments, reducing his need for one-on-one support by an educator by 50% within the next 12 weeks.

Goal 2: **Increase autonomy in communication**

Objective: Within 12 weeks, Sam will use visual aids or a communication device to express his needs and preferences in at least 70% of opportunities throughout the day, reducing behaviours of frustration and increasing engagement.

Goal 3: **Support emotional regulation**

Objective: Over the next 12 weeks, Sam will use designated emotional regulation strategies, such as deep breathing exercises or a calm-down corner, to manage feelings of frustration or anxiety. With the support of consistent and predictable routines, as well as secure and reciprocal relationships with educators, Sam will reduce the occurrence of emotional outbursts by 50% during stressful situations.

Goal 4: **Support flexible thinking in routine changes**

Objective: By the end of the school term (12 weeks), Sam will smoothly transition between activities using a visual schedule and sensory breaks, with anxiety-related behaviours reduced by 40% as observed by educators.

Goal 5: **Multidisciplinary meeting once per term**

Objective: Every three months, Sam's care team (family, key educators, speech pathologist and occupational therapist) will meet to provide updates on Sam's IEP goals, progress and modifications across the home, early learning and therapy settings. This is to ensure that everyone in Sam's care team is on the same page and able to move forward with key objectives for the next three months.

Interventions/supports

1. Whole-team approach to communication

The educators at the ECEC service adopted a whole-team approach to communication to ensure consistency in how they addressed challenging behaviours. All staff members were trained to use the same language and strategies when interacting with Sam and other children with similar needs. This consistency helped create a predictable environment where Sam could understand what was expected of him, reducing confusion and anxiety. For example, educators consistently used a calm, reassuring tone when guiding Sam through transitions, which helped him feel more secure and less overwhelmed.

2. Child-centred environment adjustments

To better support Sam's sensory needs, the educators made several adjustments to the physical environment. They redesigned the indoor environment to include more defined areas using furniture as dividers, creating quieter spaces where Sam could retreat to when he felt overstimulated. The sensory area was equipped with tools such as noise-cancelling headphones, stress balls and a sensory wall to help Sam self-regulate, and having an educator available to support with co-regulation.

3. Proactive environmental and routine strategies

The educators implemented proactive strategies to minimise the likelihood of challenging behaviours occurring. Visual schedules were introduced to help Sam and his peers understand the flow of the day and prepare for transitions. These schedules were displayed at eye level and were easy to understand, using pictures and simple words. These visuals were also made available for Sam to take with him as he explored the learning environments and refer to as needed. Sam's educators also incorporated sensory breaks into his daily routine, allowing him to engage in calming activities before transitioning to more demanding tasks.

4. Partnerships with the wider community

Recognising the need for additional expertise, the educators partnered with local allied health professionals, including a speech pathologist and an occupational therapist, to better understand Sam's needs and develop effective strategies. They provided training sessions for the staff and worked directly with Sam to implement sensory integration techniques and social skills training. The collaboration with these external professionals ensured that the strategies used were evidence-based and tailored to Sam's specific needs.

5. Involving children in decision-making

As part of their inclusive practice, the educators involved all children in the process of decision-making. Sam participated in discussions about what the children would like in their learning environments, routines and resources. By giving Sam a voice in the decision-making process, the educators helped him feel more connected to the early learning community and his peers.

Outcomes

The implementation of these inclusive practices led to significant improvements in Sam's behaviour and engagement. The consistent communication and predictable environment helped him manage his transitions with less anxiety, resulting in a decrease in aggressive behaviours. The sensory-friendly adjustments in the indoor and outdoor environment allowed Sam to participate more fully in group activities, and the regular sensory breaks helped him maintain focus throughout the day. The partnerships with external allied health professionals provided valuable insights that further enhanced the support provided to Sam, while the involvement in decision-making fostered a sense of belonging and responsibility.

Key takeaways

- Successful early intervention requires seamless collaboration among educators, families, allied health professionals and other stakeholders. A shared understanding and unified goals across settings ensure consistent and effective support for children.
- IEPs are essential tools for setting clear, actionable goals and ensuring that all strategies and interventions are tailored to meet the unique needs of each child.
- Consistent implementation of goals and strategies across different environments – such as home, early childhood settings and therapy sessions – maximises their effectiveness and reinforces support for the child.
- Embracing and implementing neuro-affirming practices prioritise autonomy, self-determination and the use of strength-based strategies to foster positive outcomes.
- Structured and meaningful goal-setting processes, followed by regular evaluations, help track progress and adjust strategies as needed. This ensures that plans remain responsive and aligned with the child's developmental trajectory.

Reflective questions for professional learning

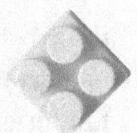

- How can you effectively collaborate with therapists and families to support children in your care?
- What are some strategies you can use to ensure consistency in implementing intervention plans across different settings?
- How can you adapt therapeutic goals to be realistic and achievable within an ECEC service?
- In what ways can IEPs be utilised to advocate for additional resources or support for a child?
- What are some challenges you might face in integrating intervention strategies, and how can you overcome them?

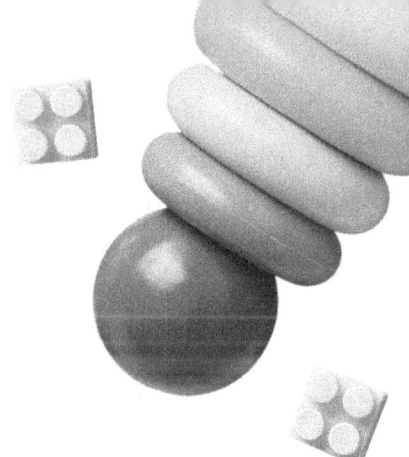

Chapter 5

Stocking your toolbox

Imagine successful inclusion as a well-organised, versatile toolbox, where the tools inside are not only plentiful, but also tailored to the specific needs of the children you work with. These tools are the strategies you've developed, the knowledge you've gained and the experiences you've accumulated throughout your career. Each tool in this metaphorical toolbox represents a specific technique, approach or resource that can be used to foster inclusion, address challenges and promote positive outcomes for all children.

Just as a craftsperson relies on a well-stocked toolbox to tackle various tasks, so too do educators rely on their own set of tools to meet the diverse needs of the children in their setting. Just as every craftsperson's toolbox is unique, so too is yours. Each team member contributes their own unique tools to the collective toolbox – tools shaped by their lived experiences, professional training and personal insights. This diversity within the team is a strength, as it ensures that the collective toolbox is rich and varied, capable of addressing a wide range of needs and situations.

Families and other professionals, such as allied health professionals, also bring their own unique toolboxes to the table. These external contributors add even more depth to your resources, offering specialised tools that you might not have developed on your own. A speech pathologist might introduce communication strategies that you can incorporate into your daily practice, while a family member might share insights into a child's preferences and routines that can help you tailor your approach.

More importantly, the children themselves also bring their own toolboxes – filled with their unique strengths, interests and ways of understanding the world. Understanding what each child brings allows you to build on their inherent capabilities and incorporate their personal tools into the broader learning environment.

Engaging in reciprocal conversations and professional development opportunities provides further chances to expand and refine your toolbox. By sharing experiences, discussing challenges and exchanging ideas with others in your professional network, you can gain new tools and techniques that you might not have considered before. These interactions not only allow you to learn from others but also give you the chance to reflect on your own practice and identify areas where you can grow. In this way, your toolbox is never static; it is constantly evolving and expanding as you continue to learn and develop as an educator.

Having a well-stocked toolbox is only the beginning. The real value comes from knowing when and how to use each tool effectively. This is where the importance of a supportive and collaborative team comes into play. When you and your colleagues work together, you create a safety net that allows you to experiment with different strategies and approaches with confidence. Your team is there to support you, offer feedback and help you refine your techniques, ensuring that you are always equipped to meet the needs of the children in your service.

Being secure and confident in utilising your toolbox can be a game changer in your journey as an inclusive educator. It empowers you to approach each day with the knowledge that you are prepared for whatever obstacles may arise, and that you have the resources you need to support every child. Moreover, it allows you to create a learning environment that is not only inclusive, but also responsive and dynamic, one that adapts to the evolving needs of your students and fosters their growth and development. By continually investing in and expanding your toolbox, you ensure that you are always ready to provide the highest level of care and education to the children in your charge, helping them to thrive in a truly inclusive setting.

This chapter will provide you with a series of tools and apply them to the running case study of Ahmed.

Case study: Understanding and supporting Ahmed

Ahmed is a bright and curious three-and-a-half-year-old boy whose family originally comes from Pakistan. Five years ago, Ahmed's family moved to Australia, and while they are bilingual, the primary language spoken at home is Arabic. Recently, Ahmed was enrolled in your ECEC service, marking an important transition for both him and his family as they adapt to a new environment and culture.

As you've been observing Ahmed over the past few weeks, certain patterns in his behaviour have caught your attention. Ahmed tends to show signs of dysregulation and overstimulation, especially as the day progresses. For instance, you have noticed that he often blinks his eyes rapidly, a possible sign that he is trying to cope with the sensory overload around him. He also tends to seek out darker, more confined spaces within the indoor environment, almost as if he is trying to escape the bright lights and loud sounds that can be overwhelming. This behaviour is particularly evident in the afternoons when the room transitions indoors after outdoor play and becomes busier with increased noise and activity due to a staggered parent pick-up, educators packing away and cleaning, and children engaging in a smaller learning environment.

When it comes to communication, Ahmed has displayed very minimal verbal language so far. He doesn't engage much in spoken communication and seems to rely more on non-verbal cues to express his needs and desires. For example, rather than asking for something, Ahmed will often take your hand and lead you to a specific area of the room to point out a resource or an item that interests him. This preference for gestures over words may be tied to his need for comfort and familiarity in a setting where the language spoken is different from what he is used to at home.

Ahmed's family members appear to be quite reserved and tend to keep their distance during drop-off and pick-up times. They don't stay around for long, which makes it challenging for you to communicate with them about Ahmed's experiences and progress during the day. Moreover, despite having access to a digital documentation platform where you post daily updates, observations and the learning diary, there has been minimal engagement from Ahmed's parents. They rarely interact with the digital platform, which limits the opportunities for you to share important information about Ahmed's development and for them to provide feedback or insights that could support his growth.

Given these observations, it is clear that Ahmed may be experiencing sensory sensitivities and challenges with communication in the new environment. His behaviour suggests that he may be feeling overwhelmed by the sensory stimuli in the room, particularly during transitions and in the busier parts of the day. Additionally, the limited interaction with his parents, both in person and via the digital platform, indicates a potential barrier in building a strong partnership with the family – an essential component of supporting Ahmed effectively.

To better support Ahmed, it might be beneficial to explore strategies that reduce sensory overload, such as creating quieter

> spaces in the room where he can retreat to when needed or using softer lighting to create a more calming environment. Also, finding ways to enhance communication with Ahmed's family, perhaps by offering in-person meetings or using a translation service, could help bridge the gap and ensure that both you and his parents are working together to support Ahmed's development.

Having the Inclusion Together Agreement resource in your toolbox

The Inclusion Together Agreement resource is a comprehensive framework designed to facilitate collaboration among educators, families and professionals in fostering inclusive ECEC environments. Originally known as the Working Together Agreement, this initiative was developed by the ACT/NSW Inclusion Agency in partnership with inclusion experts, early childhood intervention professionals and families with firsthand experience. The resource offers practical guidance and strategies to build strong, effective care teams that work together to ensure every child, regardless of their abilities or background, can fully engage in all aspects of the learning program. It highlights the critical role of clear communication, shared understanding and collaborative decision-making, providing tools and best practices to address challenges and maintain a focus on inclusion.

In Ahmed's case, where he exhibits signs of sensory overstimulation and struggles with communication, utilising the Inclusion Together Agreement can provide a structured and collaborative approach to support his development and inclusion within the early learning environment. The Inclusion Together Agreement framework encourages the importance of building a cohesive inclusion team that works collaboratively to ensure every child's participation and success.

The first step in implementing the Inclusion Together Agreement for Ahmed is to establish a clear and consistent communication strategy among all care team members, including Ahmed's parents, educators and any external professionals involved in his care. Given that Ahmed's family speaks primarily Arabic and may have limited engagement with the service, it is crucial to explore alternative communication methods that accommodate their language preferences and cultural context. This might include in-person meetings with the aid of a translator or using visual aids that can help bridge the communication gap.

The Inclusion Together Agreement also encourages the need to incorporate best practices in ECEC services, such as play-based learning and the use of natural, everyday environments. For Ahmed, this means creating a learning space that minimises sensory overload and providing opportunities for him to engage with his peers in a comfortable and supportive setting. Educators can work with the inclusion team to modify the physical environment by introducing quieter, dimly lit areas where Ahmed can retreat to when he feels overwhelmed.

A key goal to support Ahmed would be the importance of finding common ground among all care team members in the ECEC service. This could involve identifying shared goals, such as improving his communication skills or supporting his sensory needs. By engaging in open and respectful conversations during staff meetings, reflective conversations and an IEP session, Ahmed's key educators can develop a clear action plan that outlines the specific roles and responsibilities of each member. For example, educators might focus on implementing sensory-friendly strategies in the indoor environment, or they could refer to a speech pathologist that could provide targeted interventions to support Ahmed's communication development. Ahmed's parents can be encouraged to share insights from home that might inform these strategies, ensuring that the plan is holistic and responsive to his needs.

Fostering functional communication

Functional communication refers to the use of practical and effective communication methods that enable an individual to express their needs, desires, thoughts and emotions in a way that is understood by others. It encompasses a range of communication forms, including verbal language, gestures, facial expressions, visual aids and assistive technologies. The goal of functional communication is to empower individuals, particularly those with communication challenges, to interact meaningfully with others and navigate their environment successfully. It is focused on ensuring that communication serves a clear, purposeful function in daily life, helping individuals convey important messages and participate fully in social, educational and community settings.

Expanding on the concept of fostering functional communication for Ahmed involves recognising that communication is more than just spoken words – it is about finding the most effective ways for Ahmed to express himself and understand others. Given that Ahmed is still transitioning into the learning environment and may feel overwhelmed by the sensory input, it is crucial to implement strategies that not only accommodate his needs but also empower him to communicate in ways that are comfortable and effective for him.

One of the foundational strategies is ensuring that all adults in Ahmed's world – whether they are key educators or his parents – use a consistent, functional communication approach. This could involve encouraging Ahmed to use a combination of prompts, gestures and facial expressions to convey his needs and emotions. Educators and parents should be receptive to these non-verbal cues and responsive in a way that reinforces Ahmed's attempts to communicate. For example, if Ahmed points to a toy he wants, responding quickly and positively will encourage him to continue using gestures as a valid form of communication.

Visual aids are another powerful tool in Ahmed's communication toolbox. Visual routine charts, visual lanyards, picture cards and social stories can all be instrumental in helping Ahmed process daily routines, transitions and play schemas. These aids not only support Ahmed in understanding what is happening around him but also provide him with a predictable structure that can reduce anxiety and increase his sense of security. For instance, a visual routine chart that shows the sequence of activities throughout the day can help Ahmed anticipate what comes next, making transitions smoother and less stressful for him. These visual aids should not be confined to the learning environment alone; they can be equally effective at home.

Through designed visual aids that can both be utilised within the ECEC service and at home, Ahmed's parents can implement a consistent approach to communication that reinforces what he is learning during the day. This could include visual schedules for daily living activities, such as packing his bag, playing a two- to three-step game or mealtime routines. Consistency between home and school environments is key to helping Ahmed feel secure and supported, as it reduces confusion and builds a bridge between his experiences in both settings.

Social stories are another invaluable resource that can assist Ahmed with big transitions or experiences that are new to him. Social stories are simple narratives that describe specific situations (with visuals), what to expect and how to behave in a way that is understandable and relatable for Ahmed. These stories can be particularly useful in preparing Ahmed for events that might be overwhelming or unfamiliar, such as a fire evacuation drill or a doctor's visit. Reading and discussing these stories ahead of time, Ahmed can better understand what will happen and what he is expected to do, which can significantly reduce anxiety he may experience.

Furthermore, the use of social stories can be extended to the home environment. For instance, a social story about getting ready in the morning can help Ahmed understand and prepare for the steps involved in this routine, enhancing his executive functioning skills. An important word of caution: not all social stories or visual aids are neuro-affirming. What is important is supporting children to develop strategies that work for them, as opposed to teaching them to 'be neurotypical'.

Executive function skills refer to a set of cognitive processes that help individuals manage and regulate their thoughts, emotions and behaviours to achieve goals. These skills include working memory, cognitive flexibility, planning, organisation, problem-solving, impulse control and self-regulation. For young children like Ahmed, executive function skills are crucial in helping them navigate daily routines, transitions, manage sensory input, communicate his needs, adapt to new environments and engage in social interactions. For example, Ahmed's difficulty with transitions and his tendency to seek out darker, quieter spaces when overwhelmed suggests challenges with cognitive flexibility and self-regulation – key components of executive functioning. Cognitive flexibility allows children to adapt to changing circumstances or switch between tasks, while self-regulation involves controlling emotions and behaviours, particularly in response to sensory stimuli or stressful situations.

To support Ahmed in developing these skills, educators and parents can implement structured routines and visual aids that provide clear, predictable steps for daily activities. These tools can help Ahmed build working memory by reinforcing the sequence of actions he needs to take, such as getting dressed or transitioning from one activity to another. Social stories can also assist in enhancing Ahmed's planning and problem-solving abilities by preparing him for new experiences and providing strategies for how to respond.

What is sensory processing and how can it support my learning environments?

Sensory processing refers to the way our nervous system receives messages from the senses. Traditionally, there were five senses (sight, sound, touch, taste and smell); however, we now recognise the *proprioception*, *vestibular* and *interoception*. The messages received through our senses turns them into motor and behavioural responses. For most individuals, this process happens automatically, allowing them to navigate their environment smoothly. However, for some children, like Ahmed, sensory processing can be more challenging.

Sensory processing difficulties can manifest as either hypersensitivity (over-responsiveness) or hyposensitivity (under-responsiveness) to sensory input. For example, Ahmed might experience sensory overload in environments that are too loud or bright, leading to behaviours such as blinking his eyes rapidly or seeking out darker, quieter spaces to escape the overwhelming stimuli.

> ***Proprioception*** – is the sense that allows us to perceive the position, movement and action of our body parts without directly looking at them. It is sometimes referred to as the 'sixth sense' and involves receptors in our muscles, joints and tendons that send signals to the brain about the body's position in space. This sense helps with tasks such as walking without looking at your feet, typing without watching your hands and knowing how much force to apply when lifting objects.
>
> **Link to Ahmed's case study:** Ahmed's need to retreat to darker, quieter spaces and his difficulty with transitions may suggest challenges with proprioception. If Ahmed struggles to perceive his body's position in space accurately, he may feel unsteady or unsure during movement, which can be exacerbated by bright lights and loud noises. By incorporating proprioceptive activities into Ahmed's sensory diet, such as pushing or pulling heavy objects, deep-pressure (yoga) or gross motor activities (outdoor obstacle course), can help Ahmed feel more grounded and secure in his environment.
>
> ***The vestibular system*** – is responsible for our sense of balance and spatial orientation. It's located in the inner ear and helps us maintain our posture, stabilise our gaze and understand the movement and position of our head in relation to gravity. The vestibular system allows us to move smoothly and coordinate our movements, such as walking in a straight line or standing up without losing our balance.

Link to Ahmed's case study: Ahmed's tendency to seek out quieter, enclosed spaces and his difficulty with overstimulation might indicate sensitivity within his vestibular system. If Ahmed's vestibular processing is challenged, he may feel disoriented or unbalanced, particularly in busy or fast-paced environments. Incorporating vestibular activities into his sensory diet – such as swinging, rocking or spinning – can help regulate his vestibular input, providing the movement he needs to feel balanced and calm.

Interoception – is the sense that helps us perceive and understand internal bodily sensations, such as hunger, thirst, pain and the need to use the bathroom. It plays a crucial role in self-regulation, as it allows individuals to recognise and respond to the body's internal signals. Interoception is essential for managing emotions, understanding physical needs and maintaining overall wellbeing.

Link to Ahmed's case study: Ahmed's minimal communication and reliance on gestures may reflect challenges with interoception. If Ahmed has difficulty interpreting internal signals, he may struggle to express when he is hungry, tired or in discomfort. This could contribute to his behaviour of seeking out dark spaces or withdrawing when overstimulated. To support Ahmed, educators and parents can incorporate activities that help him become more aware of his body's internal cues. For example, regular check-ins throughout the day to ask Ahmed if he needs a break, a snack or a rest can help him start recognising and responding to these internal signals. Using resources previously mentioned, such as social stories and visual supports that illustrate bodily cues and appropriate responses, can empower Ahmed to communicate his needs more effectively, enhancing his comfort and participation in both the learning environment and at home.

Implementing a sensory diet across the day

A sensory diet for Ahmed would consist of specific, scheduled activities designed to provide the necessary sensory input that helps him stay calm and focused throughout the day. These activities could be seamlessly woven into the centre's routine to ensure that Ahmed receives consistent support without feeling singled out. For instance, the day could begin with a calming sensory activity, such as supporting Ahmed to start his morning with a few minutes in a designated sensory corner. This space could include dim lighting, soft cushions and sensory tools like a weighted blanket or tactile objects that Ahmed can use to self-soothe.

As the day progresses, the sensory diet can be adjusted to fit different parts of the routine. For example, during group activities or circle time, Ahmed might benefit from holding a small fidget toy or wearing noise-cancelling headphones to help him manage auditory input while still participating in the group. Transition times – such as moving from indoor to outdoor play or preparing for lunch – can be particularly challenging for children with sensory sensitivities. Incorporating a brief sensory activity, like deep-pressure squeezes or a few minutes of swinging or rocking, can help Ahmed regulate his sensory system before transitioning to the next activity.

In the afternoon, when Ahmed tends to become more overstimulated, additional sensory breaks could be introduced. These breaks could involve activities that Ahmed enjoys and finds calming, such as water play, sand play or even a quiet story time with soft background music. By aligning these sensory diet activities with the natural flow of the day, Ahmed's sensory needs can be met consistently, reducing the likelihood of sensory overload and enhancing his ability to engage with his peers and educators.

Brain breaks

Brain breaks are short, physical or sensory activities designed to give the brain a rest from cognitive tasks and allow it to reset. They are particularly beneficial for children who struggle with attention, focus or sensory processing challenges. These breaks can range from simple exercises like stretching or jumping to activities that involve sensory engagement, such as playing with textured objects or listening to calming music. For Ahmed, incorporating regular brain breaks into his day can help manage sensory overload by providing him with opportunities to step away from overwhelming stimuli and engage in activities that soothe his nervous system.

Linking brain breaks to Ahmed's case study

Brain breaks are another essential component in supporting Ahmed's sensory and cognitive needs. These short, structured breaks provide opportunities for Ahmed to reset his nervous system and refocus his attention. The care team can strategically schedule brain breaks throughout the day, particularly during times when Ahmed might be expected to focus on a task for an extended period or when he has just completed a challenging activity.

For example, after a structured learning session or during transitions between activities, a brain break might involve a few minutes of physical movement, such as jumping, stretching or a short walk outside. These activities can help release pent-up energy and provide proprioceptive input, which is often calming for children with sensory processing challenges. Alternatively, brain breaks could involve sensory play, such as exploring different textures with his hands, listening to calming music or engaging in deep breathing exercises.

By incorporating brain breaks into the overall routine – not just for Ahmed, but for all children – the service can create a more dynamic and responsive learning environment. This approach benefits all children by providing them with the tools to manage their energy levels and maintain focus, while also normalising the need for periodic rest and sensory input.

Partnerships with families

Building strong partnerships with families is essential for fostering a child's development and ensuring a collaborative approach to their learning journey. For early childhood educators, this partnership serves as the foundation for addressing any concerns about a child's development, such as any behaviours of concern or sensory sensitivities. In the case of Ahmed, who experiences sensory overstimulation and has limited verbal communication, forming a trusting relationship with his family is a crucial first step before discussing the potential need for further assessment or support from allied health professionals. These conversations can sometimes lead to sensitive topics like seeking a diagnosis or considering external support such as from allied health professionals, so it is vital to handle them thoughtfully and collaboratively.

Developing a professional relationship built on trust, respect and open communication is key to successful partnerships with families. This begins with creating a welcoming and supportive environment where families feel that their insights, cultural backgrounds and experiences are valued. For Ahmed's family, who primarily speak Arabic at home and may not engage as frequently with the early childhood service's digital communication platforms, building this relationship may require additional effort.

Educators might need to explore alternative ways to communicate effectively, such as offering in-person meetings with a translator, using the translator within the program or utilising simple visual communication aids. This approach ensures that Ahmed's family feels included and understood, laying the groundwork for productive conversations about his development.

Once a strong relationship is established, it becomes easier to engage in conversations about potential developmental concerns, such as Ahmed's sensory sensitivities or his minimal verbal communication. With trust in place, families are more likely to feel comfortable discussing their observations and concerns, leading to a collaborative exploration of support options. This is especially important for Ahmed, whose behaviours – such as seeking out dark, quiet spaces or relying on gestures to communicate – suggest he might benefit from additional support. By approaching these conversations with sensitivity and empathy, educators can then help guide Ahmed's family towards considering a more formal diagnosis or engaging allied health professionals, if appropriate.

Involving allied health professionals, such as speech therapists, occupational therapists or psychologists, can provide additional layers of support for Ahmed. Introducing these professionals to the family or facilitating their involvement within the early childhood service can be a crucial step in addressing Ahmed's needs. For families who may be unfamiliar with these services or hesitant about their involvement, framing the introduction of allied health professionals as a way to further support their child's development can make the process more approachable.

In Ahmed's case, an occupational therapist could provide valuable insights into his sensory processing challenges, offering practical strategies to help him manage overstimulation. Similarly, a speech therapist could work with Ahmed to develop alternative communication methods that align with his non-verbal cues and gestures, empowering him to express his needs more effectively.

As educators, facilitating these introductions and supporting families through the process of engaging with allied health professionals can be transformative. It allows for a more holistic approach to Ahmed's development, ensuring that his needs are understood and met across all areas of his life. Regular collaboration between the family, educators and allied health professionals ensures that everyone is aligned in their approach and that Ahmed receives consistent support both at home and in the early childhood setting.

For Ahmed's family, who may not be used to engaging with the educational service regularly, this process also opens the door to ongoing, open communication about his progress. Educators can schedule regular check-ins with Ahmed's parents to discuss any observations, adjustments or recommendations from the allied health team. This continuous dialogue helps build confidence and reinforces the partnership between the family and the early childhood service.

Goals

Step 1: Building trust with the family

Before setting any goals, it's critical to establish a strong relationship with Ahmed's family. Since Ahmed's family speaks Arabic at home and may be less familiar with the early childhood service, the first step is to create an open and welcoming dialogue. This might involve in-person meetings with a translator to ensure the family fully understands the process and feels comfortable sharing their observations. By involving Ahmed's family from the beginning, educators can gather valuable insights into his behaviours at home and any concerns they might have, such as his sensory sensitivities or limited verbal communication. Building trust ensures that the family feels like equal partners in the goal-setting process, and they are more likely to engage consistently moving forward.

Step 2: Collaboratively setting short- and long-term goals

Once the family feels comfortable, the next step is to collaboratively set short- and long-term goals for Ahmed. These goals should not only focus on his development within the early childhood service, but they should also reflect his family's priorities, and how he can be supported at home and during therapy sessions. For example, a short-term goal might focus on helping Ahmed use visual aids to communicate his needs, such as pointing to picture cards when he wants something, aligning with strategies both at home and with allied health professionals. A long-term goal could aim at gradually improving his ability to manage sensory overload during transitions or when the room becomes noisy, with consistent strategies used across the learning centre, at home and during therapy sessions.

Consider the importance of goals being clear, measurable and achievable – but ensure there is consideration of flexibility as well. For instance, educators and Ahmed's family might agree that over the next six weeks, Ahmed will strive to independently use visual aids to express his needs across the day, in times like: snack time, playtime and outdoor transitions. Long-term goals might stretch over several months, such as helping Ahmed feel more comfortable during group activities by using sensory tools like noise-cancelling headphones or creating quiet spaces for him to retreat to when overwhelmed. These goals can be aligned with interventions suggested by his occupational therapist to ensure continuity across environments.

Step 3: Building a care team and sharing goals across the team

Once the goals are established, it is essential to build a comprehensive care team around Ahmed. This team includes educators, his family and allied health professionals, such as speech therapists or occupational therapists. The care team works together to ensure that Ahmed's goals are aligned across all settings – whether it's the early childhood service, at home or during therapy. By collaborating with his allied health professionals, the team can ensure that the strategies used in therapy sessions, such as sensory regulation techniques or communication aids, are also implemented in the early learning centre and at home.

After setting the goals, the next step is to share them with all staff members who interact with Ahmed. It's vital that every educator, including casual or relief staff, understands the specific goals and strategies in place. This ensures that Ahmed receives consistent support, whether he is in a group time, free play or transitioning between different learning environments. Regular communication between the early childhood service and Ahmed's allied health professionals ensures that progress is monitored holistically, with consistent updates across all settings.

Step 4: Monitoring and adjusting the goals

Consistency is key, but flexibility is also necessary. As Ahmed progresses towards his goals, regular check-ins with both his family and the team are important. Educators should document how Ahmed responds to the agreed-upon strategies, such as how often he uses visual aids or how he reacts to sensory tools. Allied health professionals can contribute insights from therapy sessions, while Ahmed's family can share observations from home. This documentation helps track progress and identify any areas where adjustments are needed.

For instance, if Ahmed is using the visual aids successfully during snack time but not as much during playtime, the team might adjust the strategy to include more direct prompts or reinforce the use of visual aids through modelling. These adjustments should always involve Ahmed's family and allied health professionals, ensuring they are aware of any changes and that similar strategies are being reinforced at home and in therapy.

Step 5: Ongoing collaboration with allied health professionals

As Ahmed's goals evolve, it might become necessary to involve allied health professionals more frequently. These professionals can offer support, such as speech therapy to improve communication skills or occupational therapy to help manage sensory sensitivities. By ensuring that strategies suggested by these professionals are integrated into Ahmed's daily routine at the centre and at home, his care team ensures that he experiences consistent support across all areas of his life.

For example, if Ahmed's occupational therapist recommends using a specific sensory tool, such as noise-cancelling headphones during noisy transitions, this tool should be used consistently at the early childhood service and at home. Educators can also facilitate meetings between the family and therapists to ensure everyone is aligned in supporting Ahmed's development.

Funding

Inclusion in ECEC services requires a holistic approach, where decisions are made based on the needs of the child, the family and the overall learning environment. While funding can certainly support inclusive practices by providing additional resources and staffing, it should not be the primary driver behind decisions related to enrolment, resourcing or the provision of additional staff. The focus should always remain on the best interests of the child and the creation of a supportive, inclusive environment, regardless of the available funding.

In Ahmed's case, the decision to provide him with additional sensory tools, extra staffing support or communication resources should be based on his individual needs rather than the availability of funding. Whether or not extra funding is accessible, Ahmed's educators should focus on providing a consistent, inclusive environment that meets his sensory and communication needs. For example, creating quiet spaces for him to retreat to when overstimulated or using visual aids to support his communication can be done with minimal financial resources, but could have a significant impact on his experience.

In Australia, inclusion support funding varies significantly across different early childhood settings, as well as between federal and state-based services. As such, there is no one-size-fits-all approach to understanding how funding operates within early childhood. Some services may have access to federal programs, such as the ISP, which helps ECEC services include children with additional needs, while others may rely on state-based initiatives that offer support in different ways. This variability means that educators and families should focus on understanding the specific funding models available within their region and service rather than relying on generic funding information. In Ahmed's case, his family and educators should explore what specific funding options are available to support his needs, but they should never feel that funding is the sole determinant of how much support Ahmed receives.

It's important to remember that funding alone should not dictate the level of support provided to a child. For example, when considering additional staffing or resources for Ahmed, the decision should come from a genuine need to enhance his learning experience, not from the availability (or lack) of funding. Funding can be a valuable tool to help provide the right resources, but even in the absence of specific grants or financial support, educators should strive to produce a meaningful, inclusive environment by utilising existing resources creatively and strategically.

Here are some general tips for educators and service leaders when considering funding in relation to inclusion, using Ahmed's case as a practical example:

1. ***Understand your options.*** Each state or territory may have different funding avenues for inclusion support, so it's important to stay informed about the various funding opportunities available within your specific context. Whether it's federal programs or local initiatives, knowing what is accessible to your service helps you make informed decisions. In Ahmed's case, exploring both local and national funding schemes could provide additional resources to support his sensory and communication needs.

2. ***Use funding as a supplement, not a solution.*** While funding can enhance the resources and support available for inclusion, it should be seen as a supplement to your existing practices, not the solution. For example, Ahmed's sensory needs might be met through creative use of existing materials, such as setting up a quiet sensory space in the room, rather than waiting for specific funding to arrive. Inclusion should always be embedded into the service's philosophy and daily operations, with or without additional funding.

3. ***Advocate for the child's needs first.*** The primary focus of any inclusion support should always be on the child's individual needs. In Ahmed's case, if the team identifies a need for additional staff to help him during transitions or provide extra support during group

activities, the request for funding should be based on these specific needs. Even if funding is unavailable, the team can find ways to work with Ahmed's family to ensure consistency between home and the early learning centre.

4. ***Be flexible and creative with resources.*** Inclusion doesn't always require large financial investments. For Ahmed, simple adjustments like using visual aids for communication, providing sensory tools such as noise-cancelling headphones or organising brain breaks can make a big difference in supporting his sensory regulation without needing additional funds. Often, services can creatively repurpose existing resources to meet children's needs, ensuring that inclusion is achievable in any funding context.

5. ***Plan for long-term sustainability.*** When using funding for inclusion, consider how these supports can be maintained in the long term. For Ahmed, the goal should be to embed consistent practices that help him thrive, regardless of whether specific funding streams continue. By building strong, inclusive practices within the team, Ahmed's progress can be supported without relying solely on temporary financial support. Sustainability ensures that, even if funding changes, Ahmed will continue to experience a nurturing and inclusive environment.

Key takeaways

- Think of inclusion strategies as tools in a toolbox which will be continually upgraded with knowledge, experience and resources so you have a wide range of tools to support each child.
- Building relationships with families is critical to a child's success. Open, trusting communication ensures shared goals can be developed and consistency between the home and the early learning environment can be maintained.
- Understanding and supporting sensory processing needs of individual children is essential so that you can help children regulate their responses to sensory input and support their participation throughout the day.
- Inclusion is most effective when educators, families and allied health professionals work together to set clear, measurable goals for each child that are regularly reviewed, and consistent strategies can be implemented.
- While funding can enhance inclusive practices, it should not drive decisions about resources or staffing. Inclusion should be embedded in the service's daily practices, and sustainability should be the goal so that the supports provided are effective long term, regardless of changes in funding.

Reflective questions for professional learning

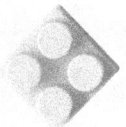

- How effectively are we building trusting partnerships with families, and in what ways can we improve communication to ensure that families feel valued and involved in their child's learning journey?
- Are the goals we set for children, such as Ahmed, consistently aligned across home, early childhood settings and allied health professionals, and how do we ensure that these goals are communicated and implemented by all care team members?
- In what ways are we using available resources and strategies to create an inclusive environment, even in the absence of specific funding, and how do we balance financial constraints with the needs of the children in our care?
- How do we, as a team, monitor and adjust individualised goals for children like Ahmed to ensure they are both achievable and responsive to the child's progress, and how do we engage in continuous communication with the care team?
- What steps are we taking to ensure that our inclusive practices are sustainable long term, regardless of changes in funding or staffing, and how do we embed inclusion as a core value in our daily operations?

Chapter 6

Building confidence and capacity in your team

There are a number of important considerations in building confidence and capacity in individual team members, and to also acknowledge the importance of the capacity of the team as a whole. This chapter outlines the importance of all individual educators feeling heard and contributing to ongoing positive practice change.

Individual educator philosophy and approaches

Everyone has their own philosophy about early childhood. This philosophy is the framework of your beliefs and values that guide your practice. As there are multiple people working in an early childhood service, it is important that everyone is encouraged to reflect on what their own personal philosophy is, that is – what their core principles are. Doing this encourages everyone to reflect on what is most important to them in their role as an educator.

Having a discussion about each person's core principles will allow everyone to feel their input is respected and it ensures that what is important to everyone becomes known. For example, one educator may really value the role of play in children's learning; another may be passionate about environmental sustainability; another may believe inclusion of every child must be reflected in all aspects of the service. Once everyone has had the opportunity to share what is important to them individually, similarities and differences can be explored.

This open dialogue allows a service philosophy to be built with input from everyone. When the majority of people share values, these seamlessly become part of a service philosophy. However, it is of equal importance that differences in priorities are explored, and each member of the team helps the others understand why something is central to their beliefs and values. A philosophy everyone has contributed to and understands is more likely to be reflected in daily practice.

Maintaining philosophy of the service

All educators having a clear understanding of the service philosophy is necessary. The service philosophy can be seen as the vision of the service, from which policies and practices can be developed and improved. Unless everyone agrees on what should be in the service philosophy, there will always be inconsistent practices. When everyone is secure with what the philosophy means in practice, it is easier to ensure that it is maintained as the foundation for all practice in the service. This often requires change – maybe to attitudes, to priorities and most importantly to practices across the service. To make any positive changes in a service, this vision needs to be clear.

As far back as 1987, Delores Ambrose developed a change management model. This model identified five crucial components to implementing any change in a sustained and meaningful way. These components included the vision, skills, incentives, resources and action plan. When any one of these components is missing, instead of resulting in positive change, other outcomes may occur. The diagram of the change management model is shown opposite, as well as the resulting outcomes when one of the five key components is missing.

Figure 5: Ambrose Model of Change adaptation

Vision	Skills	Incentives	Resources	Action Plan	=	Change
	Skills	Incentives	Resources	Action Plan	=	Confusion
Vision		Incentives	Resources	Action Plan	=	Anxiety
Vision	Skills		Resources	Action Plan	=	Resistance
Vision	Skills	Incentives		Action Plan	=	Frustration
Vision	Skills	Incentives	Resources		=	Treadmill

(Villa & Thousand, 1999)

If we focus on our service philosophy as the vision, we can see that having a clear, shared vision is needed as our starting point, but it is not enough on its own. We also need to be sure that we have the necessary skills, incentives, resources and a clear action plan to move forward. Each of these components is embedded within this text. Each different component of our philosophy can be seen as part of our vision. We can apply this model to part of our vision (or service philosophy), which is to ensure every child is included in our ECEC service. When everyone agrees that this is essential, we can work on developing our skills of inclusion, understanding how it benefits everyone, what resources we have or need to have to ensure success, and some practical and realistic steps to achieving an inclusive service. Really understanding your service philosophy means that all educators are clear on what is expected for all families, educators and any visiting support professionals in ensuring inclusion for all.

It is really important that a philosophy is a living document. Instead of the philosophy being written, displayed and forgotten about, it needs to continually be improved, updated and reflected upon. Educators may display sections of their philosophy, with frequent additions of practices which reflect those different parts of the philosophy. If reflection does not occur across the service, it is likely that the impact of the philosophy will gradually decrease, and the key components will fade away until they are not evident in practice.

Curriculum approach

At an international level, there is significant variation in curriculum approaches to early childhood. In Australia, the EYLF provides a curriculum framework to guide practice. The introduction of this framework in 2009 brought an expectation of consistent high-quality practice across all early childhood services. While there were previous quality improvement and assessment guidelines for some services, there was not one national framework that guided early childhood practice.

The introduction of the National Quality Framework has provided foundational information and expectations which sit alongside individual team values to create the vision for each service. Individual services often made decisions based on their own individual and service philosophies, but not all shared the same commitment to inclusion.

The introduction of the EYLF (and subsequent National Quality Framework for ECEC services – ACECQA, 2012) led to key principles, practices and outcomes becoming foundational to high-quality early childhood services. Having a good knowledge of the EYLF means educators are aware of how their practice reflects the principles and outcomes. While this framework must guide all decisions within ECEC services in Australia, there was still scope for interpretation. The newly updated EYLF V2.0 (2022) has more specific guidelines in many areas, including respect for diversity. Whatever guides your curriculum decisions, it is essential to recognise that any curriculum can be adapted to ensure all individual learners are catered for. Let's look specifically at some examples from the EYLF.

Principles – while all of the principles can link to inclusion, the one that is most explicitly linked is *Equity, inclusion and high expectations*. Within this principle, there is recognition that educators need to be committed to equity, they creative inclusive learning environments and adopt flexible and informed practices. These then optimise access, participation and engagement, which support wellbeing and positive outcomes. Educators are also required to make curriculum decisions that promote genuine participation and inclusion, challenging practices that contribute to inequity or discrimination (AGDE, 2022, p.17).

Practices – again, all practices are designed for all children, irrespective of disabilities, developmental delays or neurodivergence. One practice addresses *Learning environments*. Within this section, there is reference to safe and inclusive learning environments, environments that support learning and are responsive to all individual children and allow for reasonable adjustments. There is reference to collaboration with families, allowing for uninterrupted time for optimal learning, meaningful materials and the role of educators supporting engagement of all children (AGDE, 2022, p.23).

Learning outcomes – all five learning outcomes are relevant to all children within the service. Let's consider *Outcome 1 – Children have a strong sense of identity*. We know that a healthy identity is crucial in learning, development and overall wellbeing. Children need experiences where they can exercise agency and feel significant and respected. In addition, everyone has the right to feel valued, accepted and successful, so opportunities need to be provided for all children to experience these outcomes. Secure relationships help everyone feel a sense of belonging. There are a range of strategies educators can use to ensure all children have opportunities to develop a strong sense of identity (AGDE, 2022, p.30-31).

Working as a team

Early childhood services have multiple educators with varying levels of training and experience, and are often made up of a range of working arrangements, encompassing full-time and part-time roles. If we just consider the impact on a team where people have different days of employment, where sometimes everyone may not see all of their colleagues across a week, we can see the challenges this can raise for working as a team. Let's consider the following example:

You have a team of six people in your service which includes:

- One university-trained teacher who is the director with six years' experience in the current service who works full-time; this teacher has a particular interest in the physical activity of young children
- Two diploma-trained educators, one with 20 years' experience, but only one year in your service who works two days a week; they are passionate about inclusion of children with disabilities, developmental delays and neurodivergence; the other educator is Aboriginal, has two years' experience and works four days a week
- One educator who has a Cert III with eight years' experience in the current service who works two days a week; their particular interest is in Forest Schools and embedding nature programs in the service
- One full-time trainee who is excited about their role in early childhood, but has not expressed any particular interests
- One educator who has a Cert III and previously worked as a paediatric nurse; their passion is helping children who have experienced trauma.

What a diverse and wonderful team! If everyone focuses just on their own key values and interests, the diversity of experience and passion is lost. If everyone can share their values and interests, learn from each other and respect the contributions of each other, the team becomes stronger. Everyone's passions and individual experiences become embedded into the service philosophy and the diversity of the team becomes a strength.

Consider the difference when people work as individuals in the same workplace, or when they actually work as a team. In the first image opposite, everyone is individual.

Figure 6: Team development

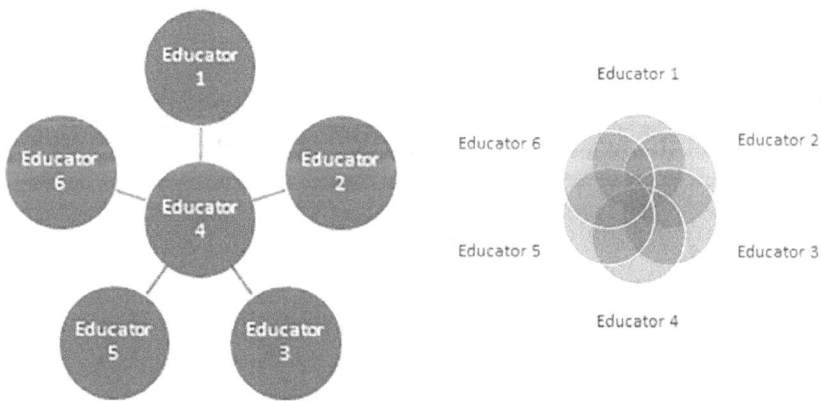

In the second image, everyone still maintains their individuality but overlaps and becomes one team. This is what each service should aim for.

Working as a team allows individuals to share their strengths and support each other during more challenging times in a service. Genuinely being part of a team creates a shared approach and is more likely to lead to achieving a cohesive service. The African proverb, 'It takes a village to raise a child' referred to wider kinship groups having a responsibility of child rearing, rather than the responsibility just falling to one parent. However, we can also apply this proverb to an early childhood service, where the early childhood service is the village with everyone working together to lead to positive outcomes in children.

Learning from each other

Every individual educator has their own strengths, but everyone needs to remain a lifelong learner. Some members of the team will have more formal qualifications, which may mean they have a stronger theoretical understanding that underpins their practice. Some members of the team might have fewer formal qualifications but have strong practical skills and a passion for education that others can learn about. Some educators may have personal experiences that enrich their practice. What is important to remember is that remaining open to ongoing learning is an essential quality for *all* educators.

We can link this to the image of the change model earlier in the chapter. Think about the need for skills and resources in this model. Without adequate skills, anxiety can increase as people grapple with whether their practices are optimal. Without adequate resources (which can include people), there is an increase in frustration, where people are wanting to uphold the vision, but lack the resources to do so. Learning from each other in our teams brings a richness to our practice, as well as ensuring agency for everyone as an important member of the service. In addition to learning from our colleagues, we can also learn from families and other professionals. Importantly, we can learn from children, which is crucial in any high-quality service. Having a service culture where individuals are recognised is important, but also allowing opportunities for everyone to teach and learn builds confidence and capacity in the team.

Building skills across all people

It is easy in services to deflect to the more experienced, qualified or confident educators. However, this will lead to some people continuing to develop skills and others never having the chance to grow. Sometimes supporting children with disabilities, developmental delays or neurodivergence can lead educators to feel a bit 'out of their depth'. In these instances, it is of course a good idea to call for additional support from someone who may have more knowledge or experience. However, rather than passing over to them, the less experienced or knowledgeable educator can learn a lot from being involved in this process.

It may be that they watch and listen, then debrief with the more experienced and knowledgeable educator afterwards. But on another occasion, it may be completely appropriate to be mentored or coached through something, to learn 'on the go'. This does require commitment and a positive, collaborative approach from everyone. There may be times when this will not work, but when it is possible, it will contribute to the increasing confidence and experienced of the person who previously found this difficult.

Let's revisit the case study of Sam from Chapter 4.

Sam is a four-year-old child diagnosed with ASD level 3 and sensory processing difficulties. Sam exhibited difficulties with transitions between activities, often leading to frustration and aggressive behaviours such as hitting or pushing peers. Additionally, he struggled to engage in group activities, frequently isolating himself due to sensory overload. Imagine Sam is playing in the sandpit, and it is time to come in for lunch. While other children are standing up and dusting sand off themselves, Sam remains in the sandpit and does not move. You go over to him and say, 'Lunchtime, Sam', and he pushes the child who is standing next to him about to get out of the sandpit. That child falls over and hurts his hand and starts crying.

You want to attend to the child who has been hurt, and you know you should also help Sam understand it is not acceptable to push peers and also encourage him to come inside. You can see, however, that Sam is becoming a bit 'heightened'. He is now hitting the sand with the spade and flicking the sand out. You feel like you are not sure what to do when his emotions start to escalate, so you call one of your more experienced colleagues. This is a good example of the change model, when someone is lacking skills, and it results in increased anxiety.

While you focus on the child that was hurt and give them your attention, you are also watching what the other educator is doing to help Sam with his emotional regulation. After you have guided the other child in for lunch, you pay attention to the language the educator is using, their voice tone, their positioning, Sam's responses and all the different strategies the educator uses. When you are on your next break, you ask that educator if you can make a time to chat about the strategies they used, the decisions they made, and how and why these were effective for Sam. This will then help you to learn, increasing your skills – so the next time a situation like this occurs with Sam, you may feel confident enough to step in. Remember that experience and confidence do not just grow overnight, but small steps will absolutely help you to get there!

Being respected by your colleagues is part of the foundation to building confidence. Encouraging each other to grow and learn will help build skills across all individual educators. This is essential for everyone individually, but also collectively to build a strong, resilient team where a growth mindset becomes part of who you are. To help everyone in the team to build their skills and knowledge can sometimes take time. Colleagues supporting each other to grow is enriching and will lead to everyone developing further skills and confidence.

Professional development

In addition to learning from each other to increase skills and knowledge, it is also important to access professional development opportunities as well. This may be specific to your own service, where you identify areas of need and then invite someone with expertise to come in and work with your team on a specific area within inclusion.

You may find local courses that can be accessed either in person or online, or even national or international conferences. These can be both a source of knowledge and provide networking opportunities which can continue to support you. When considering what you feel will help you and your service, just be sure to find reputable organisations or individuals. Check on their role in the community or their qualifications and/or experience to ensure you are getting quality, relevant, current knowledge. For example, Early Childhood Australia and Community Early Learning Australia have several courses, webinars and modules relating to early childhood; and Reimagine Australia has a range of online information sessions, webinars, modules and communities of practice supporting both families and practitioners working with children with disabilities, developmental delays or neurodivergence. These are some peak organisations that can be a starting point for your exploration of professional development.

Key takeaways

- Individual philosophies need to be shared for everyone to respect and understand each member of the team.
- Building a service philosophy provides a clear vision that guides service practice.
- Respecting each other is essential.
- Finding ways to build cohesion across the team is important, especially when there are people working different days.
- Only allowing more qualified or more experienced people to do things they are confident and competent in means they will continue to build both capacity and confidence, leaving others just 'treading water'.
- Encouraging colleagues to try new things will lead to skill development and confidence. This does not mean they are 'thrown in the deep end', but rather can work alongside more experienced people to gradually build capacity.

Reflective questions for professional learning

- What team-building experiences can you have to build a sense of belonging in all members of the team?
- In what ways can you offer opportunities for everyone's strengths and passions to be shared?

Chapter 7

Supporting transitions

Transitions are defined as "the process or period of changing from one state or condition to another" (Oxford University Press, 2024). When we transition from something we are familiar with to something new or different, a range of emotions emerge. Think about how you feel during a transition. Maybe it is moving house, starting a new job, or the start or end of a relationship. You may experience excitement, stress, fear of the unknown or nervousness about leaving something you are familiar with.

When we think of transitions in the early childhood environment, we need to think about the range of transitions that might occur, including transition into the ECEC service, transitions throughout the day, transitions from one room in the service to another and the transition out of the service to a school setting. While some of these transitions seem more significant to others, each child will respond differently and may require additional support. For children with disabilities, developmental delays or neurodivergence, transitions often require a lot more preparation, planning and consideration.

This chapter will explore ways to support an individual transition that will be successful and tailored to individual children and families.

Effective transitions into the service

The transition into an ECEC service can be overwhelming for children and their families as they enter a new world! This may be the first time parents have left their children for extended periods. It may also be the first time they have left their children with someone they are not familiar with. For example, parents may have left children with grandparents, trusted friends or babysitters, but if this is their first time in an ECEC service, it can be quite overwhelming. They may not have much knowledge of what happens in a service and may be apprehensive about whether people will really look after their children, cater to their needs and support their development and interests. This transition can be far more overwhelming when a child has disabilities, developmental delays or neurodivergence.

Let's consider two different examples of children starting at the ECEC service:

Macie is a three-year-old child who has an older brother, Jackson, who is in Year 1 at school. They are new to the area, so have never been in your service before, but Jackson did go to preschool in their previous location. Macie is meeting developmental milestones for a three-year-old child and is very talkative and social.

Tristan is a three-year-old child who does not have any siblings. Tristan does not use verbal language to communicate and becomes overwhelmed in new environments. While he does not have a diagnosis, Tristan's parents did mention during the enrolment process that they are on the waiting list to see a paediatrician as they have noticed Tristan does not seem to be doing things that other friends' or relatives' children are doing, even though some of them are younger.

Do you think the transition into the ECEC service will be the same for Macie and Tristan? What about for their families?

While of course we cannot generalise and make assumptions about how either Macie or Tristan or their families may feel, it is likely that Macie's parents are less nervous because Jackson has already attended an ECEC service. They have left Jackson with unfamiliar people at his previous service, and they have also experienced Jackson now being in school. As Macie is very talkative and social, it is likely she will develop friendships fairly easily, and she can also share with her family what she likes or doesn't like about the ECEC service and can talk with them about different things that happen across the day.

On the other hand, this is a completely new experience for Tristan and his parents. They have already identified that he finds new places a bit overwhelming. Tristan's parents may already feel a little anxious about him not being able to tell them anything about his day, whether he enjoyed it, how supported he feels and what the day might look like. They have indicated they have concerns regarding his development and may already be feeling a little overwhelmed themselves. Research has found that families whose children have disabilities, developmental delays or neurodivergence can be more anxious about leaving their child at an ECEC service (Warren et al., 2016).

What happens during the transition is the foundation for every child's sense of belonging. How supported the family feels may have a big impact on how comfortable and valued they feel in the service, and how trusting they will be of you and what you do. Transition into the service for both Macie and Tristan is really important. However, for Tristan and his family, this transition is even more significant in the foundations that are laid for his inclusion. "Transition into ECEC centres can lay the foundation for the success of inclusion in ECEC centres, which can then impact on further transitions, such as the transition to school" (Warren et al., 2016, p.18).

All the strategies you use to help children feel a sense of belonging are important for every child. For Tristan, however, there may be additional things you need to consider. For example, it is important that you provide lots of information to Tristan's parents about how you will be meeting his needs and supporting his learning. There are many ways you might support Tristan's transition into the service.

Consider the following suggestions and how helpful you think they might be:

- Have an extended conversation about whether Tristan's parents feel that shorter days may make the transition easier, or if full days are appropriate for him. They may also want to consider adjacent days if that might support Tristan to be less apprehensive or anxious.
- Discuss ways his family supports him in new environments.
- Find out about his favourite toys or interests so you can embed them into the service.
- Develop an understanding of his communication style and how his parents would like you to share things he is doing during the day (such as taking photos, developing a communication book or sending them frequent updates during his transition into the service).
- Work with Tristan's parents to develop goals and discuss family priorities.

As you have more time to observe, and get to know Tristan, you will understand these things. However, having these conversations early will ensure that you are setting Tristan up for success in the new environment, and also help to alleviate some of the concerns his parents may have.

Transition throughout the day

Some children, just like adults, can transition easily from one experience to another. But transitions during the day can be particularly challenging for some children for a range of reasons. Consider a child who might be experiencing sensory sensitivities. Changes throughout the day might be overwhelming for them and can also challenge educators.

Understanding each child and the things that might trigger them to become overwhelmed are important. When a child first starts at the service, they may be coming from a home environment where there are very few big transitions. They may have been able to make decisions about how long they can play with chosen toys or activities, they may eat when they are hungry and can move freely across the day based on their own needs and interests. While it is ideal for children to have large blocks of uninterrupted time to engage in their chosen play, an ECEC service will have a routine that has been designed a certain way.

If food is provided at the service, mealtimes may need to be more rigid based on when a cook has prepared lunch. Rest time may be designed based on a limited number of educators available at that time, or there may be a range of factors that contribute to the routine a service has developed.

These things all need to be taken into consideration, but it is important not to have transitions just for the sake of transitions. Ask yourself, do all the children have to move from one thing to another at the same time? Reflecting on why you have a particular routine is important, but it is also important to consider the individual children you have in the service each day. For some children (like Tristan), there may need to be more preparation for changes throughout the day.

Some useful strategies to consider might include:

- Using a timer to help children prepare for a change
- Having a particular song or chant that signals that a change is going to occur – such as a pack-up song, or a song that is sung when all the children are going to be preparing to go to lunch
- Using a visual timetable to outline key parts of the day so that all children can visually see that after outside time, it will be time for morning tea

- Developing some social stories that address different parts of the day that can be read during the day or even be sent home for children's parents to read to them to develop an understanding of different parts of the day in the ECEC service
- When a child such as Tristan is demonstrating success in one of the aspects of these transitions, you may ask them to be a leader of that activity. For example, 'Tristan, would you like to go and get the sunscreen for us, please?' and 'Tristan, that was such beautiful packing away; would you like to be the line leader to afternoon tea?'
- Reflect on other additional resources that might support children like Tristan.

One thing that is essential to remember, is that not every child has to always be doing the same thing at the same time. This does not mean we are not having expectations for all children, but each child is an individual and that needs to always be at the forefront of our minds. However, having a predictable, yet flexible routine will help children develop security in what happens across the day.

Preparation to transition between rooms

In a long day care service, children may move from the baby room to the toddler room to the preschool room as they grow. Transition from one room to another can be as overwhelming for a child or family as the transition into the service, as they navigate a new environment and sometimes less familiar educators. While you may think a child is familiar with the service and they might be able to manage these transitions, a new room can have new educators, new routines, new expectations and a whole new sensory environment. Again, think about the preparation that can occur to make this more seamless for everyone. Would some of the following strategies help?

- Consider whether there is an opportunity to rotate educators for short bursts; for example, having educators from the room the child will be moving into 'visit' the child in their current room. The visiting educator could share a story, be part of mealtime or just be part of the current routine so that the child can become more familiar with them.

- Integrate educators from other rooms into your routines – you may wave to them through a shared glass window or door, you may introduce the educator as they walk past, you may comment about something specific you know about that educator that is also a common interest or a pertinent topic in your room.
- If the children share time in the playground, for example, encourage the less familiar educators to spend time engaged with the child in play so the child starts to feel comfortable with them.
- If there are particular toys or experiences that are in the other room, consider sharing those across the rooms so the child becomes more familiar with those.
- Have 'visits' with the child to the new room at times that are the easiest for the child. For example, if they have difficulty engaging in group times, avoid visiting during group time. If they find loud noise difficult, select a quieter part of the day to visit.
- Make a social story with photos of different experiences, the physical environment and the educators who will be in the room to read for an extended period leading up to the transition.

These are just some things you can consider, but you may already have other ideas that will work effectively in your service to assist in transitions between rooms.

Supporting parents with transitions outside the service

Open communication with parents is always beneficial. If you are having success with a child who is finding transitions difficult, make sure you share with parents any strategies that are working well for their children. This may assist parents in supporting their children in transitions across other parts of their life. For example, a parent may be finding it difficult to transition their child in and out of the car or transitioning to bedtime. You can share strategies with the family, such as visual supports, timers, preparation or transition objects, that we previously referred to.

It can also help parents with going to different places. These may be familiar places (like grandparents' homes or swimming lessons), or less familiar places (like the doctor's or a large shopping centre). While you may think familiar places are more secure for children, there can still be different smells or sounds that can be difficult for a child without preparation. For the less familiar places, creating social stories or even just discussions can help. Remember, though, that while parents know their children best, and they may already use some strategies that work, they may still appreciate some new ideas or options to consider.

Transition to school

The ECEC service will hopefully become a place of security and support for all children. While they might have settled into the service well, considerations about how to effectively transition children to school are really important. There is a lot of great information available about the transition to school, and the essential role of preparation and planning. For all families, they may need support about their local schools, and expectations of school. Reimagine Australia has a wide range of resources available to support children, families, educators and schools with the transition to school. These free resources include practical information to support each of the stakeholders to ensure each child is supported in their transition. Preparation needs to start early. The more complex the child's needs, the earlier this planning needs to start.

Let's consider another example. Max is a three-year-old child in your service who has cerebral palsy. What this means for him is that he is unable to verbally communicate, and he uses a wheelchair for mobility. He has some movement in his arms, but restricted fine motor ability. Despite the physical challenges Max faces, he loves being around other children, and while it is difficult to assess, you and his parents all agree he is very aware, and cognitively you believe he would be understanding everything other children his age do. You know he has an older brother at his local school and his parents have mentioned they would love him to be at the same school as his brother. His parents have asked your thoughts for school in two years' time.

The first key part of this example is that his parents would like him to be at the same school (their local public school) as his brother. Remember at the start of this book where we explained children's rights? It is absolutely Max's right to go to his local school, and it is the school's responsibility to have Max at that school. When Max's parents (or any other parents) ask your thoughts, it is important to remind them that your thoughts are how you can assist in making the transition to the school of their choice the easiest, and most seamless for both Max and them. There may, however, be times when a parent has a child with disabilities, developmental delays or neurodivergence, and they are unsure of options that might be available for school, and they really want your opinion (or more often your guidance) regarding different options. In those cases, *provide families with options – but remember it is not your choice.*

There are a number of different school options available to children with a range of disabilities, developmental delays or neurodivergence. Importantly, parents should be able to choose. It is the educators' role to provide families with options and support the process. In Australia, different states have different options. However, currently in New South Wales, children with disabilities, developmental delays or neurodivergence can be enrolled in different environments depending on their particular learning needs. These include:

- *Mainstream school* – may be public, private or independent. Personalised planning and adjustments are provided to ensure the child is included in the classroom with their peers.
- *Support classes in mainstream schools* – these have smaller numbers and are available for students with moderate to high learning and support needs. There may be specific classes for

autism, behaviour disorders, mental health difficulties, cognitive delay or sensory impairments.

- ***Specialised schools*** – for example, Schools for Specific Purposes (SSPs) are specifically for children who require high levels of support; and Aspect (Autism Spectrum Australia) schools are specifically designed for children on the autism spectrum. Both these schools have a strong focus on developing life skills as part of the curriculum, to assist students to become as independent as possible.

While the choice should be made by parents, they may need support in both understanding different options, and in the preparation process. Here are some ways you can support them:

- Become familiar with some of the options in your local area.
- Offer to visit some of the options with the family if they need or want extra support.
- Find out who the contact person is for the different options, so you can assist parents in starting the planning.
- Be open to sharing information you have about the child (of course, with parent permission), with any school representatives coming to visit the child in the service. A more collaborative approach to transition will always lead to a smoother, easier transition for children and their families.
- Work with families on specific transition strategies that may assist their child (which we will discuss in the final section of this chapter).

If we go back to Max, the family already has one child in the school, so they should first have a conversation with the school about what they want. Importantly, in Max's situation, the school may need to make modifications if they have not had a child using a wheelchair in the school. The school will then contact the Department of Education to start the process of funding so that modifications can be made prior to Max starting. As Max is not independent in his movement or self-help skills such as toileting and eating, he will also be eligible for support which the school will apply for. Other things to consider include:

- Creating a 'This is me' book, or a story or video to introduce Max to the school if they are comfortable doing so
- Helping other people understand the importance of inclusion – this should not just be up to the parents to be the advocates
- Asking Max's parents to discuss with the school the sort of communication book you have used or what system they feel would work best for them in the school. Be willing to chat with the school to support Max's transition.

Here are some key tips you can share with families:

- Know your rights.
- Review your options.
- Work out what you want.
- Have as much information as you can to support you.
- Contact the school and meet with the principal – don't be afraid to take a support person.
- Be open and honest when filling out paperwork (the more honest you are, the most appropriate supports can be determined).
- Get therapists and/or doctors involved.

Practical ways to support children to transition out of the service

There are many practical strategies that can support children to transition more effectively into school. Remember that all the transition strategies you use across the service for other children will also apply to children with disabilities, developmental delays or neurodivergence. There may be a few other things you could consider that might support the other strategies you have implemented with all children.

Consider some of the specific skills a child might need, such as opening a lunchbox, sitting to listen, wearing a uniform, packing their bag, lining up, waiting their turn, sitting in a seat for specific periods of time, listening to different bells to know what the upcoming transition is or using bubblers/taps/new toilets. Most children will need these, but for some children, more preparation may be needed for these skills.

If we consider a child with sensory sensitivities, something like wearing a school uniform can be the thing that makes the transition the most difficult. The material may be different to something they have previously worn, there may be 'scratchy' tags, socks might be thicker or the shorts less flexible. While most children will adjust to this fairly easily, a child who is hypersensitive to touch may find these things excruciating.

Prior to the child starting at the school, you can encourage parents to drive the route to school regularly, point out the school, have their child practise wearing the uniform and, if useful, develop social stories. Ask the school about its orientation program and whether parents can practice with their children some of these steps. The more preparation, the more these things can be worked through before the child starts at the school.

Key takeaways

- For children with disabilities, developmental delays or neurodivergence, the transition into the service lays the foundation for inclusion.
- Transition into the ECEC service can look different for different children.
- Parents should always be involved in transition decisions and processes.
- Transitions during the day can be difficult for some children, who require additional support.
- Transition to school for children with disabilities, developmental delays or neurodivergence is complex and requires preparation and planning.

Reflective questions for professional learning

- What are some of the things you might speak about with a parent of a child with disabilities, developmental delays or neurodivergence before or as the child starts, to support the transition into the service?
- If a child is struggling with transitions during the day, what strategies do you think you could use to support them?
- If you have a child in the toddler room with sensory sensitivities who is moving up to the preschool room, discuss ways you could make this transition easier.
- Even if you have a comprehensive transition to a school program in your service, discuss additional considerations for the transition of children with disabilities, developmental delays or neurodivergence.

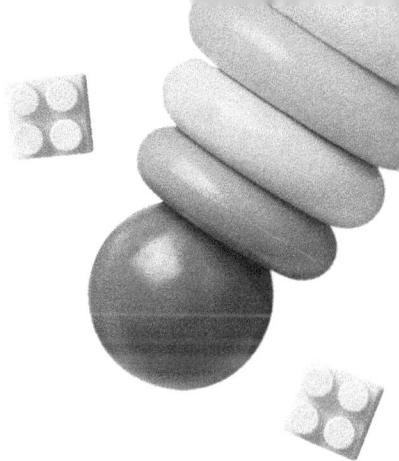

Conclusion

Being an early childhood educator is one of the most important jobs in the world. Children's brains are the most malleable in the first five years of life. Everything you do makes a difference. It is not just about the difference you can make for children with disabilities, developmental delays or neurodivergence. It is about the difference you can make in developing inclusive attitudes in all children, so they are more aware, more accepting and more understanding. Difference is just difference, and it should never be seen as a deficit. It is important all educators know that inclusion is about similarities and differences. It is important to understand that all children deserve to have their needs met, but also that needs vary based on each child.

We know there are hard days, and we have both experienced those! Our goal was just to share our knowledge and experience, and we hope that there are some tips you have picked up that will help you in your journey to becoming a more inclusive educator. We hope our philosophy was clear – that all children and families have rights, and everyone deserves to feel a sense of belonging to their family, their early childhood service and their community.

Here's one final tip: don't expect to suddenly feel fully equipped to manage all situations. Just like your initial early childhood training gave you a good foundation, it is your experience, watching others, making mistakes and learning from them that helps you every day to become a better educator. Working with children with disabilities, developmental delays or neurodivergence can sometimes leave you questioning whether you know what you are doing. From our experience, we have felt this many times, but instead of deciding it is too hard (which is clearly not an option!), we have delved into our toolbox, spoken to more experienced colleagues and practised. If you can drive a car, you know you had to start somewhere. If you can swim, you know your first time in a pool was not diving in and swimming laps. Small steps will lead to big gains.

Our hope is that you use one thing from this book that helps you and keep practising that. Once you feel a bit more confident, pull the book out again and find another thing that you can do. Over time, you will realise you have stocked your toolbox. You will not only be a more inclusive educator, but you will also be a role model for other educators. It is only when we all work together that we can change the culture of the service. Only together can we ensure that all children and families truly feel valued and that they have all the opportunities the wonderful world of early childhood services can offer.

Useful resources

ILP
NSW Department of Education template
https://tinyurl.com/327kvwy2

Observation styles
Gowrie NSW
www.gowriensw.com.au/thought-leadership/observation-in-childcare

Tips for using visual supports
NSW Department of Education
https://tinyurl.com/c3vx7s9y

Communication tools
National Autistic Society UK
www.autism.org.uk/advice-and-guidance/topics/communication/communication-tools

Antecedent, Behaviour, Consequences (ABC) recording
NSW Department of Education template
https://tinyurl.com/bdetd89f

Thrivary digital tool for collaboration
www.thrivary.com.au

References

Australian Children's Education and Care Quality Authority (ACECQA). (2012). *National Quality Framework.* www.acecqa.gov.au/national-quality-framework

Australian Children's Education and Care Quality Authority (ACECQA). (2018a). *Developmental milestones and the Early Years Learning Framework and the National Quality Standards.* www.acecqa.gov.au/sites/default/files/2018-02/DevelopmentalMilestonesEYLFandNQS.pdf

Australian Children's Education and Care Quality Authority (ACECQA). (2018b). *National Quality Standard.* https://www.acecqa.gov.au/nqf/national-quality-standard

Australian Disability Network. (2024). *Definition of disability.* https://australiandisabilitynetwork.org.au/

Australian Government Department of Education (AGDE). (n.d.). *Inclusion Support Programme.* www.education.gov.au/early- childhood/inclusion-support-program

Australian Government Department of Education (AGDE). (2022). *Belonging, Being & Becoming: The Early Years Learning Framework for Australia (V2.0).* Australian Government Department of Education for the Ministerial Council. https://www.acecqa.gov.au/sites/default/files/2023-01/EYLF-2022-V2.0.pdf

Australian Government Department of Social Studies. (n.d.). *The Australian Parenting Website.* Raising Children Network. https://raisingchildren.net.au

Australian Human Rights Commission. (n.d.). *United Nations Convention on the Rights of Persons with Disabilities.* https://humanrights.gov.au/our-work/disability-rights/united-nations-convention-rights-persons-disabilities-uncrpd

Berk, L.E. (2024). *Child Development (10th ed.).* Boston, MA: Pearson.

Curtis, D., Carter, M., Lebo, D., & Cividanes, W.C.M. (2013). *Reflecting in Communities of Practice: A workbook for early childhood educators.* Redleaf Press.

Curtis, D.J., Weber, L., Smidt, K.B., & Nørgaard, B. (2021). Do We Listen to Children's Voices in Physical and Occupational Therapy? A Scoping Review. *Physical & Occupational Theory in Pediatrics, 42*(3), 2022. https://www.tandfonline.com/doi/full/10.1080/01942638.2021.2009616

Davies, D. (2011). *Child development: A practitioner's guide (3rd ed.).* Guilford Press.

Department of Education, Employment and Workplace Relations (DEEWR). (2009). *The Early Years Learning Framework for Australia: Belonging, Being and Becoming.* Canberra, ACT: Commonwealth of Australia.

Doyle, O. (2020). The First 2,000 Days and Child Skills. *Journal of Political Economy, 128*(6), 2067–2122.

Early Childhood Australia. (2016). *Statement on the inclusion of every child in early childhood education and care.* www.earlychildhoodaustralia.org.au/wp-content/uploads/2014/01/Statement-of-Inclusion-2016.pdf

Epstein, A.S. (2014). *The Intentional Teacher: Choosing the Best Strategies for Young Children's Learning (Revised ed.).* NAEYC.

Garg, P., Ha, M.T., Eastwood, J., Harvey, S., Woolfenden, S., Murphy, E., Dissanayake, C., Williams, K., Jalaludin, B., McKenzie, A., Einfield, S., Silove, N., Short, K., & Eapen, V. (2018). Health professional perceptions regarding screening tools for developmental surveillance for children in a multicultural part of Sydney, Australia. *BMC Family Practice, 19*(1).

Healthy Trajectories. (2022). *Best Practices in Early Childhood Intervention: Towards Effective Implementation.* https://healthy-trajectories.com.au/wp-content/uploads/2023/01/6.-Best-Practices-in-Early-Childhood-Intervention_A-Position-Paper-.pdf

Kuper, H., Monteath-van Dok, A., Wing, K., Danquah, L., Evans, J., Zuurmond, M., & Gallinetti, J. (2014). The impact of disability on the lives of children; cross-sectional data including 8,900 children with disabilities and 898,834 children without disabilities across 30 countries. *PLoS One, 9*(9).

Marenus, M. (2024). Howard Gardner's theory of multiple intelligences. *Simply Psychology.* https://www.simplypsychology.org/multiple-intelligences.html

Mozolic-Staunton, B., Donelly, M., Yoxall, J., & Barbaro, J. (2020). Early detection for better outcomes: Universal developmental surveillance for autism across health and early childhood education settings. *Research in Autism Spectrum Disorders, 71*, 101496.

National Scientific Council on the Developing Child (2007). *The Science of Early Childhood Development: Closing the Gap Between What We Know and What We Do.* Retrieved from https://developingchild.harvard.edu/resources/report/the-science-of-early-childhood-development-closing-the-gap-between-what-we-know-and-what-we-do/

NSW/ACT Inclusion Agency. (2024). *Inclusion Together.* https://inclusionagencynswact.org.au/about/inclusion-together

Oxford University Press. (2024). *Oxford Dictionary.* Oxford University Press. https://www.oup.com.au

People with Disability Australia (PWDA). (2021). *PWDA Language Guide: A guide to language about disability.* https://pwd.org.au/resources/language-guide/

Reimagine Australia. (2016). *National Guidelines: Best Practice in Early Childhood Intervention.* Retrieved from https://reimagine.org.au/practitioner/what-is-best-practice/

Reimagine Australia. (2024). *Inclusion in practice.* https://reimagine.org.au/practitioner/inclusion-in-practice

Royal Australian College of General Practitioners. (2018). *Guidelines for preventive activities in general practice (9th ed.).* East Melbourne, Vic: RACGP.

Squires, J., & Bricker, D. (2009). *Ages & Stages Questionnaires®, (3rd ed.), (ASQ®-3). A Parent-Completed Child Monitoring System.* Paul H. Brookes Publishing Co. https://agesandstages.com/about-asq/why-screening-matters/developmental-screening

United Nations. (1989). *Convention on the Rights of the Child.* www.ohchr.org/en/instruments-mechanisms/instruments/convention-rights-child

Villa, R.A., & Thousand, J.S. (1999). *Restructuring for Caring and Effective Education: Piecing the Puzzle Together.* Adapted from the work of Delores Ambrose. https://leadingdifferently.com/tag/change

Warren, J.D., Vialle, W., & Dixon, R.M. (2016). Transition of children with disabilities into early childhood education and care centres. *Australasian Journal of Early Childhood, 41* (2), 18–26.

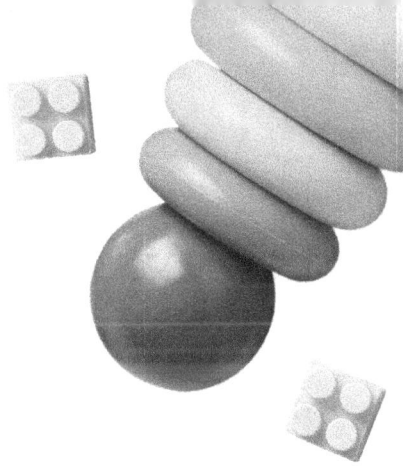

About the authors

Dr Jane Warren is a senior lecturer in early childhood at the University of Wollongong. She brings a unique blend of practical and academic expertise to the field of early childhood education, drawing from her experience as both a preschool practitioner and supported playgroup facilitator. Her research focuses on the inclusion of children with disabilities in early childhood education and care services, with particular emphasis on fostering collaborative relationships between parents and educators within an ecological framework. Jane's commitment to children's rights and her dual perspective as both academic and practitioner positions her as a distinctive voice in inclusive early childhood education practices.

Blake Stewart is a seasoned professional with more than a decade of experience in early childhood education and early intervention, currently serving as director of engagement at Reimagine Australia, which leads lead nationwide initiatives to embed inclusive practices into national frameworks. His expertise spans across education, health and disability sectors, with a focus on creating holistic, family-centred supports for children with disabilities, developmental differences or neurodivergence. An accomplished teacher and published author, Blake has taught at several prestigious universities, and his contributions to the field have been recognised with the National Excellence in Teaching Award (2019).

www.ingramcontent.com/pod-product-compliance
Lightning Source LLC
Chambersburg PA
CBHW050252120526
44590CB00016B/2315